Eating Me Alive

*How Food, Faith and Family Helped Me
Fight Fear and Find Hope*

By MATTHEW TESSNEAR

Copyright © 2019 Matthew Tessnear

All rights reserved.

ISBN-13: 978-1-7337965-3-8

First Edition: May 2019

Scriptures included in this book are from the New International Version (NIV) of the Holy Bible.

The names of products, media titles and other organizations and individuals herein are merely references and do not in any way imply those entities' endorsement of this book, nor the author's endorsement or opinion of those mentioned.

Cover Photography and Design by Matthew Tessnear
Editing by Molly A. Phipps Tessnear

For my wife Molly, my mom Chris and dad Terry, and my grandparents Harry, Lee, Lois and Vember, who have all given me life through love, faith and food

CONTENTS

Introduction: My Name is Matthew, and I have anxiety.   1

Chapter 1: Seeds of Fear and Food   13

Chapter 2: Hard Labor and Cheeseburgers   25

Chapter 3: The Prison of my own Brain   41

Chapter 4: Signs of Struggle and Support   61

Chapter 5: From Hopeless to Healing   77

Chapter 6: A Connection to Calm and Comfort   93

Chapter 7: I am still here, and I will be all right.   101

Afterword   115

Let your gentleness be evident to all. The Lord is near.

— Philippians 4:5

AN INTRODUCTION:
MY NAME IS MATTHEW, AND I HAVE ANXIETY.

I stood six-feet, four-inches tall and weighed more than three-hundred pounds. And I was terrified—of everything in the world.

My grandmother Vember, a woman of five-foot-four at her peak, always said she didn't think anyone would ever mess with me because of my size. Grandpa Lee agreed, and he always pretended to swoon when he felt the flexed muscle of my forearm. They had no idea that the old adage of "the bigger they are, the harder they fall" was not only true of me, but that my size didn't keep people away as much as it seemed to beckon people with smaller statures to constantly challenge my toughness.

Most people chuckle when I tell them I remember being one of the smallest people in my kindergarten class. Maybe I was actually quite normal in size at that time. I know my birth weight of seven pounds and six ounces, and my length of twenty-one inches, wasn't anything abnormally large. But that first year of elementary school was the last time I truly remember being small enough not to stand out. That was before I grew what most people refer to as "man boobs." It was the final year I can't remember my belly poking my much-preferred loose-fit T-shirts out a bit. I liked them loose because that gave a lesser indication of my actual shape. But at my first self-awareness of my body, I hadn't yet started dressing in an effort to conceal my size, which became an obsession of mine for many years afterward, all the way into adulthood.

Eventually, I couldn't hide behind multiple shirt and jacket combinations anymore. I was evidently what many people would call fat, and numerous people took opportunities to point that out, either bluntly or with a minimal amount of tact that didn't really veil their condescension for my keen observational obsession. And the larger I got, or felt I got, the more nervous about it I became. And the more nervous I got, the more I'd sweat. I just thought it was a physical problem, but I'd come to learn much later that it was a psychological signal as well. Even as an adult in my early thirties, I'd cross my arms to try to hide the protrusion of my large chest from my shirt, and by doing that I'd trap heat in my armpits and create sweat stains that I'd try to hide the rest of the day, in meetings and in encounters with people in all places. It was a daunting task to cover up my fat and my sweat, like trying to cover holes in my appearance, only to see more pop up by the minute, like one of those old comedy bits where there's a leaky pipe, and covering one hole just makes water spout from another.

My mother has never liked the word fat. At one point I believe she told me I couldn't use it. I know she said to never call her or any other female "big mama." She had her own weight concerns at a young age. Then she had me and got skinnier due to the stress of being a parent and a wife and a church volunteer and all sorts of other things for which she never really received full credit. That's the life of a mother, it seems. A mom's job titles are endless, and so is their stress, but the praise is light. I'm not a female, so I can never be a mother, but I understand what weight, both physically and mentally, can do to a person, as well as the rarity of appreciation. More than anything, I get what intense self-pressure and a low self-image can do to a person. For the record, I've never called anyone fat. Well, no one other than myself.

Food gets all the credit, or blame, for my size. I grew up in a

Southern, church-going family. That's all you need to know to surmise that we all loved to eat. At least for a couple generations, we appreciate home-cooked food and lots of it. Don't start to picture images of Professor Sherman Klump's family in "The Nutty Professor" movies starring Eddie Murphy. We don't waddle up to the table, plop down and eat the world until we're unable to get up between meals. We just like to eat. We appreciate good food. And we're a line of people who know how to cook and cook well. We also don't waste anything we cook, so that means we eat it all until the last morsel is gone from the plate. We don't clean our plates because someone makes us. We clean them because we love the food, all the way down to the crumbs.

Maybe our love comes from the fact that many of our favorite recipes derive from family favorites passed down through multiple generations. And we're proud of that history and our competency for preparing meals the way our beloved ancestors did. But somewhere along the way I began using food as a tool to deal with my health. And it made my health worse. It became a sort of warped kryptonite that I had no power against. Life hands us great ironies like that, seemingly taking something or someone we love deeply and turning it against us. My family would likely say the devil himself is the one who makes that happen. And I'd agree with that.

I remember thinking somewhere along the third grade that I was disgusting. To be totally honest, I recall the very precipitant of that line of thought. During a bathroom break from my elementary school classroom, I retreated to the restroom and shut the door on the stall. There was no lock on any of the stalls in that restroom—an issue that continues to persist decades later on men's bathroom doors and one which I actively campaign about on social media, in verbal conversation and in any other medium in which someone might listen. With my pants fully down and my business in progress, one boy opened the door and another poked his head under the stall wall, and they both pointed at me and started to laugh. They yelled out, "Look at Matthew, he's taking a s***!" Other boys started to huddle around my little hole in that room, which I remember being illuminated by sunlight coming through the dirty, finger-print-covered windows. It was the only bright place in the school at the time because the whole place was dark while under construction. I felt like I was on display for the whole world to see, like those dreams about being naked or on the toilet that people have, only mine had come true as a living nightmare. Embarrassed doesn't begin to describe my red complexion. My heart hurt. I was mortified, and I've never recovered from that moment. Not even a little.

From that day forward, I've had a strange relationship with bathrooms. They've become my least favorite but most important room in every building I enter. I pray every dwelling has a clean men's restroom with an open door, locking stalls and walls that leave as little gap for peepers as possible. My home state of North Carolina has sadly become known to many for the infamous 2016 "Bathroom Bill" about gender rights for restrooms. While I think the whole situation was regrettable due to the poor light it shed on the state, which is actually quite pleasant, and its inability to successfully navigate a contentious issue, I understand the core of the argument at hand. No pun intended. A restroom should feel like a safe place for everyone, no matter where and when and who and how. I believe that with all my heart because since that day when I was nine years old, no bathroom has felt safe to me, a heterosexual natural-born male. I'm as vanilla a person as they come. Yet, I always need a safe restroom because I have Irritable Bowel Syndrome.

Many people make fun of IBS, as it's called for short. Adults are the worst. I realized that when it became the topic of jeers and sneers during a meeting at a former employer. But it's no laughing matter when your stomach sends you to the bathroom sometimes ten to twenty times in a day. You can do things to help control a stomach impacted by IBS, but you can't fully escape it, especially when your mind kicks into full gear with stress and fear. And those feelings are the biggest aggravators for my IBS. They all have a very close and complex relationship. I'm certain I showed signs of struggles with my stomach and my mind before that day in third grade. Actually, I know it. But that's the major point of reference in my life—that mockery in the elementary bathroom—when I first recall my mental and physical health being related and being in a very poor state.

Fearing to go to the bathroom in public, because I knew I couldn't guarantee doing it safely and privately, caused me to change how I ate. But none of my approach even makes sense because I reacted in two different directions. For years, I would eat very little and become very persnickety about what foods I would eat, especially if I had to go to school, church, or to a restaurant the next day, where I might encounter other people in a bathroom. On the other hand, I would absolutely binge on as many snack foods as possible in times when I knew I'd have days without having to likely use a public restroom facility. I'm certain, looking back, that those overloads of food didn't help my IBS problem. And I know without a doubt that they contributed to my eventual obesity.

There's a popular story in my family that involves me hiding behind the bed as a child eating crackers. We had plenty to eat in our house, and my mom always served up a delicious homecooked meal, but I would try to sneak a snack any time possible. Mom and dad would both go out of the house for a bit for a walk, and I would hop into the kitchen, open a pack of crackers and down them as fast as possible. Or in later years when they could leave me at home alone, they'd both be gone and I'd bounce into the kitchen and devour a half box worth of oatmeal cookie snack cakes with cream filling and then jump back into my room or the den. Whatever I could quickly get my hands on, I would throw down my throat. I would deprive myself of food all week—hoping to keep my system clean and not have to use the restroom in public—and then when I knew I had a day or two when I wouldn't have to worry about it, I'd eat anything and everything I could. These habits at a young age set the stage for similar activity as I got older, and the pattern grew to a point when my food consumption began to have a direct connection to my mental and physical health.

So, the bathroom and the kitchen have always had an odd connection for me. As much as I loathe the memories of the bathrooms of the world, I have always seen an escape in the kitchen. I've thought of it as the place where I can drown my troubles, sometimes in pain and sometimes in comfort. If there's always food available, and I grew up with more than enough to eat, then I always had a vice by which I could focus my frustration about other problems. The more stressed I became, the more I ate. And the more food I consumed, the more weight I gained. And the more weight I packed onto my body, the more I worried about the way I looked and the possible bathroom needs I'd have in public. Over the years, I had no idea just how much of a connection all these pieces had to one another, and how fixing or altering one might enable me to improve all of them.

Not until I was thirty-two years old did I begin to make these connections and change my outlook on bathrooms and kitchens, on my body and how it should navigate both rooms. Actually, I think it was the next year, after I turned thirty-three, that I really came to understand myself and how I should navigate a home or other building. That better perspective came following a decision to put any kind of a career on hold and focus entirely on my health, at the urging of my wife and the complete confusion or misunderstanding of almost everyone else I knew. A man who lives in traditional society is supposed to be a breadwinner and the foundation of the household, especially monetarily. It's still unheard of in most typical social and occupational circles for a male to stop working to stay home and work on his life, unless he's experienced a complete upheaval, caused by something like drug abuse or a terrible physical accident. But I hit the pause button on my life to stop running the rat race, and then I hit rewind to start thinking backward through years of fresh yet intentionally blurry physical and mental anguish. That process caused more physical and mental pain, but it also helped me remember why I felt so poorly at an age still relatively young. And I hoped taking a break from chasing down career and financial goals would eventually lead me to a state in which I could resume a more normal life.

That normalcy hasn't returned yet. And let me be the first to tell you that it won't, at least not entirely. No matter how much I still feel the weight and heat of the expectation that a man should get up and go to work on a schedule with the main goal of increasing his earning power and bringing home the bacon to his family, it's not the model that works best for me, no matter how many people keep asking when I'm heading back to the grind. I've realized by stepping away from the office environment that there's more to life than securing a fancy job title, packing a resume full of impressive promotions and pleasing a group of people who are all grasping for their spot at the top of the ladder no matter what it takes and how much it affects others. I need something different, and I finally know why. It's a big thing with a little name: Anxiety.

Most people think Anxiety and anxious mean the same thing. I'm here to tell you they do not. Anxiety is a constant, chronic, serious condition that causes a person to fret about literally everything. Being anxious, on the other hand, is a temporary state of concern about a situation. For most of my life, I thought I was just anxious, worrying and fearing certain things that often made me more nervous than the next guy. Somehow, I missed the day in school or at work when there was a test to help me realize and understand that my condition was far more severe than a simple passing fret. I have Anxiety. *My name is Matthew, and I have Anxiety.* The first time I gained the reasoning and strength to say that was a big day in my life. Likely, it was a moment that no one else completely noticed. Sometimes that's how big days go.

So, what does anxiety have to do with all my musings about bathroom fears and food binges? I'm getting back to that because, after all, that's the whole point of this book that I'm finally, after so much thought and recollection, sharing with you. Food and fear have always had a deep connection in my life. I guess I could say my life is pretty F'd up! Get it? Ha! But seriously, I have stayed away from food because of fear, and I have pursued constant food consumption because of fear. In both approaches, I've damaged myself, and I eventually reached a very low point at which I pretty much pulled myself completely out of society as a whole. I became a modern hermit, afraid to leave the house and encounter anyone other than my wife and parents in any context.

A doctor or counselor might tell you that my pulling inward and out of social situations almost altogether was an unhealthy move. I'm certain family members thought I was spending too much time to myself and that I should get out of the house more. And maybe that's true, at least in part. But I've always known that my best method of thinking has been to isolate myself, spending lots of time getting myself "back to center," remembering who I am and who I'm not. A lot of that process comes through writing. Fortunately, during a period of more than a year with a lot of alone time, I've come to realize that the kitchen, and physically spending time there, has been a huge part of my life. The only catch is that I've had to completely change my relationship with the kitchen and with food as a whole to massively alter my life.

Instead of seeking food as a companion by which to drown my Anxiety, I've come to know culinary pursuits as a means of therapy by which to handle my mental health challenges. In the past, when I had a bad day at school or work, I'd run home, open the cabinets and start eating anything I could find. That was especially bad news when I lived by myself as a post-college bachelor for a number of years before meeting and marrying the love of my life. Or I'd go out to a restaurant and get takeout that I'd mow down in a matter of minutes, or even sometimes seconds. Once, I ate more than one-hundred shrimp in a restaurant challenge. I ate a whole takeout five-dollar pizza one night—a move I regretted the next day when I was sure I was having a heart attack from the indigestion the pizza caused. Then there were the binges of whole bags of nacho cheese chips and entire boxes of snack cakes. If you name it, I probably ate it, especially if it was high in calories, fats, sugars and preservatives. And, gosh, my body started paying for it. I gained weight by the tens of pounds and started to experience pain throughout my body. It was like I channeled every mental ill in my life into harming my physical health. When I stepped back from a stressful decade-plus of my young working life, I realized just how much my mind and my body ached. My poor health, something my wife had already been able to see from her perspective, became more evident to me. And it was because I knew it was something that deeply worried my wife that I realized I needed to make a major overhaul of myself.

I've always believed that one of the most important realities in a person's life is that we must constantly reinvent ourselves, both for the times in which we live and for our own needs and situations in life. When I got married, I was no longer the sole person whose life depended on my existence. I now truly believe two people who get married each bring fifty percent of a person to a relationship that forms one person as a whole one-hundred percent. My wife was part of me now, and my poor approach to life resulted in a dwindling health that hurt her mind, body and soul, too. That was the major driving force behind my need for change. And seeing her sadness at my ailing mind and body was enough to prompt me to realize I needed to listen to her advice: leave that anguish-causing job behind and focus on yourself for a while. It was a difficult thing to do when I felt the societal expectations of being a man weighing on me. But it became evident that my wife's needs were far more important than the views of the rest of the world, even other people I care about. This realization was also the first time I truly understood just how much my wife had become priority number one in my life. I'm still working every day, because I'm never perfect, to cement my understanding of that truth, but that was when it became incredibly clear to me.

So, I stopped working, and I started walking. At first it was a mile or so a day, then two and then three, sometimes up to five or six. The consistency of physical exercise became a very important part of every day, but I knew that it wouldn't make any difference unless I changed my relationship with the kitchen, the way I saw, thought about and ingested food. No longer could I eat like there was no tomorrow, and without the typical stresses of lots of people surrounding me in a stressful office environment, I didn't need to any longer. I could eat what my body really desired, what it actually needed, yet still allow myself to enjoy food that I had loved all my life. That's a difficult balance to strike for a boy who grew up in a family of food lovers in the South. But I've reached a point of being able to manage the reality that I'm both a foodie and a person who holds many risk factors for obesity and other life-changing health conditions. In doing some recent family research and examining death certificates of ancestors, my wife and I noticed just how many of my relatives died of heart-related diseases.

Stroke has been prevalent among close relatives on both sides of my family tree. So has diabetes. And those aren't the only health issues my people know well. Many of these problems have heredity to blame, at least partly, but diet and exercise, or at least one of the two, probably have the most impact on them. There's still a solid chance I'll have to deal with at least one of the challenges others in my family have faced, but I realized at thirty-three years old that I wanted to do what I could to prevent those harsh situations, while still enjoying food, something I've always and will forever love.

So, I made a change in my mind and in my body. And while I will always be working on my overall health, chiefly the Anxiety and my battles with weight, I have learned so much from reflecting on my journey that I think could have tremendous benefit for other people. Enter this book. I am excited, and no longer embarrassed, to share some very personal stories with you about the relationship between food and fear throughout my life. And, along the way, I will share two other important words that tell my story and also happen to start with F: faith and family. So far in my time stepping away from society's typical flow, I've come to understand that food, fear, faith and family are the four words that most tell my story and maintain utmost importance to the real man I am. And I'm willing to bet that at least one of those words, either the prevalence of it or the absence of it, tells at least a small part of your story as well.

As a boy who grew up looking forward to family meals after church on Sunday afternoons, I eventually arrived at the point in which I came to believe that my life story is best told as part memoir and part cookbook. It might seem like a rather odd premise, but almost every phase of my life has been linked to food, family, faith and, unfortunately, fear. That's why I've decided to share some very personal and reflective stories with you through the lens of a guy who still, after losing more than a quarter of his body weight and no longer tipping the scale above three-hundred pounds, loves a good meal. I'm no longer binging on snack foods like I did in my days as a teenager and later a single, working young adult. Now, I've come to better understand how food should be enjoyed, and I've zeroed in on how much I enjoy the tradition of the cooking practice, as well as the eating. There's as much therapy for me in preparing food, and seeing my wife enjoy it, as there is in consuming a feast myself. And that's why I am excited to share the recipes, some from the innermost parts of my family box, that have come to symbolize hope and healing in my life. They connect my past, present and future. I don't remember the date, but I know that one of the most important times in my life was when I stopped using food to harm myself and started using it to heal myself. And that's what this whole story, told through vignettes about important people and experiences in my life, is all about.

I invite you to pull up a chair, maybe a box of tissues, because there will be passages that are difficult to read, and an appetite to learn about food and fear through a full plate of the few simple things that make me who I am at my core. Thank you for being who you are and for choosing to read about my life. I truly believe it's a story that contains pieces of many other people's journeys who have experienced similar circumstances, challenges, trials, triumphs and joys.

Matthew T. Tessnear

SEEDS OF FEAR AND FOOD

Some of my earliest memories are of waking up early in the morning in my grandma and grandpa's house in their old textile mill community of Caroleen in Rutherford County, N.C. For such a small woman, my grandma certainly had one of the loudest—and most unintentional—wake-up calls there ever was. She had a tendency to mill around the house while it was still dark outside, straightening a cushion here, moving a knick-knack there. But what really clued a person in that she was awake and that it was still early was the sound of pots and pans and cabinet doors clanging and banging in the kitchen.

My usual bedroom quarters, and the very bed I slept in, shared a wall with the kitchen, so I always had a chance to experience all the noise a short distance away. Meanwhile, my grandpa would still be "sacked out," fully asleep on the other end of their house. I'm sure Grandma had no idea how much noise she was making. The woman could sleep through the roar of a passing freight train, so I'm certain it didn't occur to her how much commotion she could produce.

Grandma didn't just bang kitchen implements together as she buzzed through the house. She also did quite a bit of talking to herself, whispering, humming and her own special non-electronic form of beat-boxing. Our family has always discussed the talents of Grandma's entire branch of the family. We believe they could've been a Partridge Family-type group if they'd had the right exposure and promotion. They all sang, danced, told jokes, a combination of the three or more. Grandma certainly had her own niche, particularly playing the piano by ear for years without any instruction until after her retirement from mill work, as well as singing in the church choir. But I think it's her humming and whispering that stands out to me most. Her tunes were always happy, downright joyful, so much that the memories are fond when I hear my wife humming around the house today. So it was a noticeable and striking difference that her pace of walking around the house and her whispering to herself often seemed so labored and fearful, not pleasant like the tunes in her heart and out her throat.

My grandmother was an incessant worry wart. I don't remember a time when she was one-hundred percent carefree and not concerned about something to a great degree. When things were tough, she'd worry about them. When things were going well, she'd find things to worry about. That sounds so much like me. I'm positive when I say that some of my earliest seeds of anxiety were sown through heredity, inherited from my grandmother. She passed them along to my mother, and they, in turn, came to me.

When I'd stay a few days with Grandma and Grandpa during my childhood, she'd often drive me about twenty minutes up the road to a fast food joint to get a breakfast biscuit and to watch people. It really didn't matter what they were doing—and often they weren't doing anything at all interesting—but she loved to watch people. I wonder if it was her enjoyment of people-watching that helped convince her that people were always watching her and listening to her. If we were out somewhere and I'd say something about someone, just an observation even, she'd shush me. The same reaction would happen in her house if you'd attempt to discuss the mere existence of anyone else. She didn't want them to hear. And, boy, she really thought someone was listening on the telephone if the line ever popped during a call, though I'm told that particular quirk is common among people in her generation because they grew up using "party lines," a bygone concept where multiple houses were connected to a single phone line. Grandma was the epitome of nervousness, so much so that when she'd get in the car to drive us for a biscuit and people-watching session, she'd implore me to be "real quiet" and still as she adjusted her seat and backed out to head up the road. If I have an ability to be peaceful while someone is driving, Grandma helped instill it. She needed complete calm to move an inch.

So, it saddens me to know that things were always the opposite of calm in her head. Eventually, in her seventies, she started showing signs of Alzheimer's, and that's what eventually took her life at the age of eighty-eight. Her daddy lived to ninety-six, so we knew she might enjoy a long life. I do wish she could have really enjoyed it more, though. When I'd wake up at the sound of her kitchen concert those early mornings, I'd get a notion to sneak out and tiptoe behind her to surprise her. I did that once when she was in the laundry corner of their garage, and I scared her so much she followed me inside, where I'd run to hide, and she popped me on the rear end. It really did hurt her more than it hurt me, because she was upset about that for a long time, the spank not the scare. But it hurt me to see the troubled look on her face when I'd thought about sneaking up on her while she was circling the house, adjusting things in the day's earliest hours before dawn. Her whispers seemed scattered. Her humming occasionally paused as she stopped to consider something in her sights or in her hands. As a child, I wondered what was going on in her head. Now, I know without a doubt she had the earliest moments of confusion, accompanied by whatever was worrying her at the moment.

Grandma was one of the most Christ-believing women I've ever met. She always encouraged me to trust in the Lord for His strength and my welfare. Her Bible and devotional books were always at arm's reach from her living room rocking chair. And most of the favorite songs she'd hum or play on the piano were old-timey hymns she'd learned as a young girl. Grandpa gave her a piano once, and I remember her sitting there playing it, looking into the mirror behind it and singing. Years later, in her final days, she sat beside my mother at a piano in front of a mirror in her Alzheimer's care unit, still in love with music. Those good family memories won't ever leave me. Yet I grow sad that all of that didn't keep her from worrying her brains out. I've wondered, especially since her passing in 2017, about the connection between anxiety, depression, fear, worry—everything in our mind—and dementia-related diseases like Alzheimer's. Grandma certainly experienced both spectrums, worrying when she still had solid memory function and worrying when she didn't. I've spent much of my life freaking out about every little thing, so will I have the same fate? I'm not sure, but it's something else I fear. Grandma certainly was a living case study.

Obviously, my grandmother's story included more than markers of mental health troubles. All those times shuttling me to breakfast at her favorite place in town indicate just how much food was important in our relationship. But like many of my family friendships that included food, it was the homemade stuff that really resonated then and now. Grandma made amazing biscuits, my favorite anywhere at any point in my life. They weren't at all like most biscuits you'd find anywhere. Small and oddly shaped, they were crispy on the outside and soft on the inside, and I swear they were so good they hopped right off the plate she turned them onto from her baking pan. We actually called them "Hoppy Toad Biscuits."

After I'd let Grandma know I was awake, usually frightening her a bit to do it, as she was easily startled when she thought she was alone, she'd shift her mind away from the worries in her head and to the cooking of breakfast. That meant someone also had to pry Grandpa from his slumber, and that task usually fell to me. Grandma would make her biscuits and fry up bacon—the crispiest bacon I've ever eaten—right in the microwave on a simple plate. The whole mealtime operation needed Grandpa's presence for the other half, the scrambled eggs and grits. He could make wonderfully fluffy eggs that had just the right amount of moisture to still call them scrambled.

They almost seemed to be mixed well yet still have a runny, yolk-like consistency. My wife would have loved them because she loves fried eggs for the runny yolks. And she would have loved his grits, too. They were so creamy, a perfect marriage between water, ground corn and butter. My grandparents' breakfast creation was a fifty-fifty partnership, a real analogy to how any good marriage should be overall.

In my younger days, breakfast at Grandma and Grandpa's house usually meant it was Saturday morning, because that was the only day they were both off and not headed to church. So that also meant I was likely leaving their house early to go down to my Dad's family homestead to work on home projects. We cut trees in a wooded area to prepare for a future family house. We painted his childhood house and mowed the grass around it. Once a week or so, we spent a day working there to keep the place in shape and to dream for the future. The thing was, like you'd expect from a child, I didn't buy into the dream my parents had to one day live there. And I certainly didn't buy into the work it took to make it happen. Even while staying at Grandma and Grandpa's, I'd fear the coming of Saturday morning because it meant it'd be time to pull on my old clothes that could get messy and get to work. Manual labor wasn't my favorite, but looking back now I think it was the overall mental strain from my anxiety about everything that kept me from enjoying the opportunity to learn about hard work and how to be handy around the home. All week I'd fret about Saturday, even when I was basically staying in my grandparents' bed-and-breakfast and knew I'd get a great homemade Grandma and Grandpa meal before the day's work began.

When I was a child, I had a tussle with both asthma and allergies, and both often threw me for a loop. If I ran too much or overexerted myself to the point of breathing hard, I'd start wheezing and eventually feel like I couldn't catch my breath. I remember one time pushing a wheelbarrow up a small hill and feeling like someone was standing on my lungs, kicking them with their heels. For a moment, I felt like something was strangling me. It frightened me so much I still think about it when I push a wheelbarrow or see that little hill, which now doesn't seem like much of a hill at all as I've aged and grown.

With allergies, I often got an itch in my nose that could cause dozens—or even sometimes hundreds—of sneezes at a time. Then I'd feel so nasally clogged that again I worried I wouldn't be able to breathe. Mowing lawns and encountering the dust, pollen and grasses associated with the task wasn't a friendly relationship with my allergies. I often worried, because of prior bad experiences with these allergens, that I'd experience another issue and not do a good job helping out my parents with the tasks at hand. So, I'd worry all week about going in the first place. And that would often keep me from looking forward to the wonderful meal my grandparents would cook me at their house beforehand, if I was staying there a day or two to spend time with them.

That usually didn't keep me from enjoying the food in the moment though. Grandpa and I would sit down to a feast, complete with jams, coffee for him and juice for us both. He'd let out this beautiful bellowing chuckle from behind a satisfied smile every time we'd eat breakfast, when I'd split one of Grandma's biscuits to sandwich egg and bacon, and sometimes grits, between the two pieces. I've always had a love for taking my bread and making a sandwich from other ingredients on my plate. Somehow, I think that habit started at the breakfast table at my grandparents' house all those years ago. My wife and I still have that dining table in our home now—and I'd have a hard time letting go of it. More than a place to just eat food, it's full of memories like those laughs and Grandma's biscuits.

I greatly regret not asking Grandma more questions about her biscuits and how she made them. At the time, I was more worried about my stomach and my allergies and all the other things I had floating around in my little head, to think much about recipes and cooking. By the time I had the deep interest in her baking or any of her cooking, she'd lost the memory of even how to cook, let alone the ability to relay how she made anything she did by hand so tasty.

In her later years, the best she could do was open up a few cans, pour them into pots and serve them to my grandpa. It was sweet, really, thinking about her trying to continue to serve her husband of nearly sixty years with a filling meal. Unfortunately, by that time, Grandma had forgotten that multiple kinds of beans on one plate doesn't make the most exciting or varied meal. Grandpa wasn't a huge fan of bean, bean and bean plates, but that was probably even more the case because of all the fond memories he had of Grandma's amazing food. Even after he had a stroke, my grandpa loved to eat. And Grandma's phenomenal cooking abilities likely played a major role in stoking that fire. I know it has made mine roar.

As much as food, faith and family were major parts of my grandmother's life, fear also played an instrumental role. I believe difficult relationships in her lifetime were part of it. Growing up poor, as most people in the South in the 1930s did, no doubt also played a part. The typical environment of the textile mills in which Grandma and Grandpa worked, very hard labor in one way or another for years on end, certainly couldn't have helped. I believe Grandma's career in mills, which started as a teenager when she quit high school to help her family of two parents and six siblings make ends meet by going to work, took a mental toll on her. Her working life is one of the earliest family historical examples I've seen of how economic struggle, psychological weight and mental health go hand in hand. The challenges throughout her life seemed to add up, those experiences never leaving her brain, and I identify with that now as I'm older and have encountered more people and more situations in life. It's difficult to let go of trying times and trying people we meet. And I believe that single struggle was a roadblock for Grandma being able to clear her mind and be at peace.

One of my final times with Grandma came when she was in the Alzheimer's unit of a care facility a few miles up the road from where my wife and I lived at the time. That afternoon I spooned small bites of an orange sherbet-like ice cream into Grandma's mouth. It took many, many bites to empty the little plastic cup, but every once in a while, Grandma would smack her lips a bit and let out a hearty mmm, with a tilt of her head and a wink of her eyes. That's how we knew it tasted good, and that's how we knew Grandma was still inside, despite the horrifying impact of Alzheimer's. Sure, there were plenty of fearful moments by then. She couldn't dare look into a mirror without seeing herself and getting upset. There were plenty of pains and perceived ills that plagued her, but she had lost her ability to relay and describe them to us. But she still had her family, especially the constant visits and care by my mother, until the very end. And she enjoyed food most of the way, too. Actually, her food has never ended.

It's rare we eat a meal in our home and I don't think of my grandmother. Her worrisome nature has had a profound impact on my life. But so has her faith in God and her love of family, as well as her biscuits and all her other cooking masterpieces. We talk about her food often, and we still use one of her cookie sheets and many other cooking utensils from her kitchen years ago. That's how we keep her alive and with us, the food and every time we recite the twenty-third chapter of the book of Psalms, which is marked at her burial place in remembrance of her. As much as the scripture means to me, I feel a certain kinship with baking and eating that keeps her in my life every time I reach for a mixing bowl or lift a piece of hot biscuit to my mouth. I'm almost certain she's still milling about, maybe even in our house now, moving things into place here and there, humming, preparing for breakfast on Saturdays, one of my and my wife's favorite meal times each week. Only, now, I believe she's in a place where she's not whispering and pausing in a worrisome manner any more. Regardless of what I face in my own mind in the future, I hope I can reach that same place, where the memories of family and food are strong, and the fear is gone.

FOOD FOR THOUGHT

Recipes that have helped make me who I am
Every recipe has a story behind it. My favorite recipes help tell my story.

Vember's Hoppy Toad Biscuits

I lament not studying Grandma's cooking with a more studious approach. The mental traditions of her work in the kitchen are some of the fondest memories of my entire life. Thinking about her food produces feelings of great peace in my heart. But as I watched her bake, I never talked to her about her methods, her inspirations or her recipes. How could I have omitted such a simple action that's so deeply tied to who I am as a Southerner and a foodie?

In the months following my realization that I battle anxiety and have all my life, I got a hankering to recreate my Grandma Vember's biscuits with her daughter, my mother Chris. Here's what we remember, mostly from my mom's recollections of the process by which Grandma made her family-famous biscuits. We call them "Hoppy Toad Biscuits," I imagine because they hopped right off the plate she served them on.

What you need:
- 2 cups self-rising flour
- ¾ cup buttermilk
- ½ cup shortening

What you do:
1. Go ahead and preheat your oven to 500 degrees. Biscuits bake best at a high temperature for a short time.
2. Add your 2 cups of flour to a large bowl.
3. Once your oven warms your stovetop a bit, stick a medium-sized metal cake pan or a pan with straight sides on a burner on top. (I like to use a cast iron pan.)
4. Take your hand and scoop out about a half cup of shortening. (Grandma used Jewel brand back in the day, then Crisco, but I

am partial to store-brand products when the quality is just as good.)
5. Rub your shortening-filled hand across the bottom of your pan on the burner. This will grease your pan and help brown your biscuits on top. (Because you will turn them over onto a plate when they're done.)
6. Put the remaining shortening in your flour in the bowl, and you should still have a good bit as you don't need much in your pan to grease it.
7. Mix the flour and shortening a bit with your hands.
8. Make a well in the center of your flour and shortening bowl.
9. Start to slowly pour in your buttermilk, and work the mixture together with your fingers in the middle of the bowl.
10. Clean off your fingers, and add the dough that's sticking to them to your mixture.
11. Once you end up with a soft dough, pinch off pieces and roll them into balls in your hands.
12. Place each dough piece in your pan until you've filled the pan and/or used all of your dough.
13. Take your fingers and press down on each piece of dough to flatten it into more of a biscuit shape.
14. Cook your biscuits on 500 for about 10 to 15 minutes, depending on your oven's heating abilities.
15. Remove the pan and turn the biscuits onto a plate. Grandma always used a paper plate, which she placed on the table when it was time to eat. She'd make her biscuits last of everything in the meal, so they'd be hot.
16. These biscuits are delicious with butter, a jam or other spread, or as a sandwich for a piece of meat, eggs or another topping.

Chocolate Gravy

Another great topping for hot, fresh homemade biscuits is what we always called Chocolate Gravy, a decadent chocolate sauce that can also be used on pound cake, ice cream or anything else you want to deck out with a little sweetness. I've even thought it would be delicious served alongside a tray of strawberries. Grandma made her chocolate gravy with biscuits, but I also distinctly remember her serving gravy over a plain cake she poked holes into. The gravy seeped down into the cake, making for quite a divine treat.

What you need:
- 2 cups milk
- 3 tablespoons cocoa
- 3 tablespoons all-purpose flour
- 1/2 cup hot water
- 2/3 cup sugar
- pinch of salt

What you do:
1. In a saucepan, mix the sugar, cocoa, flour and salt.
2. Add hot water, and cook over low heat until dissolved.
3. Add milk. Cook until thickened.
4. Serve over homemade biscuits or anything you desire.

HARD LABOR AND CHEESEBURGERS

My father's always told me he's a "hard man," a lot like his farmer grandfather Gifton McCombs. I've always taken that to mean he subscribes to the beliefs that hard work is the way to go in life and that a good dose of stubbornness, specifically not being a pushover for others, is important. I can't speak for anyone else, but he's certainly held up his banner on those stances when it's come to my life. There's not been a time when Dad has been willing to sacrifice his convictions for the profit of anyone else. In that, he's a real model of the old "sticking to your guns" cliché, and that's fitting because Dad grew up a hobby hunter in the North Carolina foothills. Throughout life he's always enjoyed a good Western film, but guns aren't the only reason that's the case.

Dad woke me before sunrise on most Saturdays when I was growing up to take me to the family homestead where he grew up, with the goal of preparing a place for him and Mom to retire someday. In springs and summers, we mowed the grounds and applied fresh coats of paint to the buildings. In falls and winters, we sawed and removed trees to prepare a place for a new future house in a beautiful spot tucked away in the woods. Throughout the year, we kept up the place as needed. None of this work, when I was a child, meant much to me. I must be transparent and make that perfectly clear. How can a kid appreciate a long-term goal such as that? If a kid appreciates much of anything at all—really understands its value—then you've got someone very special and unique. At one time, I'm certain I didn't show my thanks for anything. My parents have, with much grace, admitted that such a reaction is normal for most children. But that's always bothered me, feeling like I long squandered the opportunity to be grateful for all they've provided for me throughout the years. After all, Dad's hard work in the nuclear energy industry helped save money that, teamed with my academic scholarships, helped send me to college for an undergraduate degree.

But it may be his staunch insistence on holding onto the family land that has been and will become the greatest gift of all. Because as I've aged, I've come to understand the value of that property, not just as a family landowner opportunity, but as a meaningful piece of our heritage and ancestry. And I hope it will always be a part of our family's future, no matter what lies after the lives of me and my wife. I believe age and a little perspective from going through challenges in my twenties and early thirties have led me to really prize the fact that we own that land. It's not a symbol of great wealth or prosperity, but it's a reminder of the hard work of the people who have come before me and a testament to the bond of family that has already been passed down through the ages. Those acres have been in our family for at least one-hundred and twenty-five years, and I hope they remain so for at least that much longer.

As much as that's true now, it's also true that I absolutely loathed the place when I was a boy. In my mind, I knew it as "The Dust Bowl," a place that had more rocks to stumble over and more clouds of grainy sand-like particles floating through the air when a lawnmower or leaf blower roared than any place I've ever seen in my life. And that description is still true. It's quite the rocky, dusty place. Now, though, I've come to see those factors as fitting realities that are reminding links to the past, when the hard struggles of Depression and World War II era farming were what that land and its surrounding plots saw. There's a quaintness to the location in the country, but there's also a vast history of activity and sacrifice that I would've seen if I had been present in the past. No doubt I feel connected to the people I'm related to but never met through that place. And I have my father to thank for that, more so with every year that passes. We are so blessed to have that opportunity, most of all because of the time we've spent together there over the years. That time is something I started appreciating a few years back, before time started moving forward and leaving behind a chance to relish being in each other's presence. So many weekends of my youth were spent in the hills and hollers of the family farmland, and I'm lucky I learned through the sacrifices of time to be there, and through the challenges of youth and adulthood, to begin to prize what the place means to all of us.

Dad expected a solid effort with any task we went to accomplish when I was a kid, and he always instilled in me that doing things the right way the first time meant you wouldn't need to waste time doing it over again and you wouldn't need to worry about the quality of your work. That really stuck with me all through school and when I got into my career in journalism. Maybe I allowed it to stick too much because that approach always meant I mentally labored over every little detail, trying never to make any mistakes. That part of the equation was by no means the fault of Dad. I just took his "do it right" and "make it last" teachings too far, to the point of never allowing my mind to be satisfied or relaxed with any job. In school, I expected no less than a one-hundred on every test or assignment. When I started working, I expected to hit a home run on every project, every story I wrote as a reporter and every newspaper we released when I was an editor. Anything less than perfect was a failure on my part, no matter who made the faux pas, if there was any faux pas to begin with, and that led me to degrade myself when anything was less than ideal in its final result. I did myself a lot of harm with that mentality, and I advise everyone else to consider adopting a "do your best and leave the rest, because there is no such thing as perfect" mentality instead.

Now, years later, I believe my insistence on perfection was some kind of combination of my personality traits, all of which I can now see I inherited from family members. There's no doubt in my mind that I am direct kin of my parents and all my grandparents because I've seen their actions and reactions replicated in my life. It appears to me that my requirement of myself to be flawless was some combination of my dad's stance on doing things right and my grandma's insistence on worrying about everything. I put the two tendencies together, so I again blame myself for the erroneous approach that's harmed my mind and body over the years through the torture of stress. But I think that may be where it all came from. We all have worries and we all have expectations for our performance and our very lives, but we take it too far when we take ourselves to the woodshed over every little thing we don't do with flawless execution. No human being can live up to those standards. And I certainly couldn't either. Yet, I've often found myself completely anguished over not being able to achieve perfection, so much that I've literally bashed myself over the head and knee many times when I've come up short in my estimation.

In addition to the mental self-abuse of expectations, I've levied some pretty harsh beatings on my body, one of my worst habits. Often, when other people have let me down and I've dealt with the consequences of public failure, I've turned to hitting myself in private in a frustrated personal rage. Few people have witnessed these self-attacks, and I'm thankful more haven't seen them happening. I've never taken to cutting myself in my depression and anxiety, but I have absolutely nailed myself in the temples of my head and across my knee and given myself punch-shots in the arms as releases of anger over issues. Back when I worked in newspapers, there were many times when I wrote stories no one else would take, often taking on more than I could realistically handle in a given day or week, and considering I was doing more than my fair share, we'd still have mistakes in print, and that upset me. Regardless of the fact that I was pulling my weight, and comparatively I weighed a lot physically, I allowed myself to take on the slack of others, and when errors would occur, I'd internalize them as entirely my fault, even if I couldn't have possibly done more to prevent them. That's the personality combination I've shared previously. My dad's expectations and my grandmother's worrisome nature somehow translated into a self-madness that led me to strike my arms. I've never had any desire to hurt others, but I have absolutely had the inclination to ping myself hard enough to remember what it feels like and not make the same mistake again.

Obviously, that kind of reaction to life's lemons is completely incorrect. God teaches us throughout the Bible that our body is a temple and that we are to respect it. By doing so, we are also honoring and respecting Him. My tendency to strike myself seems pretty crazy and ridiculous on the surface, but there's a deeper problem there, a disconnect in my brain that I think I'm accomplishing something through that type of self-punishment, when in actuality I'm not doing anything good at all. Only bad things occur when we degrade ourselves. The more we do it, the more we'll keep doing it. And the more we look down on ourselves, the more we'll think others are looking down on us, whether they actually are or not. I've seen my own lofty, impossible expectations impact my perception of what others expect me to achieve.

That was never truer than when I was in school. My parents always expected me to try my very best. They didn't set any goals beyond that, that I remember. I didn't have to make As, not for their approval and pride. But I expected myself to get an A on every single assignment that crossed my desk. If I didn't, I immediately deemed it a failure, though far from an actual F. When I had a long-term substitute teacher one year during elementary school, I received a report card one term with a C on it. I had never made a C before, and I was angry that we had only had four grading opportunities during that period. I was irate. On the way home from school the day report cards were doled out, I told my mom I was going to kill myself. I actually made that threat in the car on the way to the house. Of course, I was absolutely out of line in saying or thinking that. I shouldn't have even suggested such a crazy thing. But I was dead serious, no pun intended. This was yet another example of internalizing every single error, whether my doing or someone else's, and applying torture as punishment for anything short of perfection. If I remember correctly, several complaints by parents of kids in that class led to changes in grades, and I think I eventually got a B, which I wasn't pleased with but was better than a C. Still to this day I have never made less than a B as a final grade, and while I am proud of that, I've come to realize that nobody else in the world remembers that record. Students, no one but you cares about a perfect score or academic record years later. Few occupations—outside of maybe medical programs—require the highest of marks. So, give yourself some slack, and don't panic when you don't ace everything in sight.

My dad never gave me any indication that he thought I was underperforming in schools. He wasn't too pleased the few times early on that I got in trouble for poor behavior. In kindergarten, I made a few missteps that netted pink slips, and I just remember a stern warning that that kind of result wasn't going to be tolerated. There was nothing like any message in the sitcoms on television where a kid gets in trouble for bad conduct and then gets threatened by his father with the outcome of being shipped off to military school. Dad believed in discipline at home, and that was enough to get me to behave well in public, including at school. Honestly, a little more discipline in homes would do our world some good. A person really picks up on the parenting, or lack of, that he or she receives from an early age. I might be hard on myself, but I've always taken the approach that no one else will ever have to tell me how to act, and no one will ever be able to claim or prove they're tougher on me than I am on myself. In truth, I've been way too hard on myself, but I still believe that's better than going through life not caring about how I treat my opportunities and how I treat other people.

Much to my relief, Dad has mellowed out just a bit over the years. He still has a high-strung determination to really do a great job on everything he sets out to accomplish, and that's a good thing. He and

I are so much alike, including in our expectation that machines perform properly when they're adequately cared for, and that remains a challenge for both of us—not melting down when a man-made object breaks or malfunctions. But he's absolutely evolved to being able to know when good enough is good enough. I've seen that progression in him, and I'm glad he seems to realize that he does the best he can and should eventually call it quits on a project. If Dad doesn't know already, he'll know now that I'll always see him as the hardest working man in the world. Nobody puts more thought, planning and effort into anything. I might come close on things I really set my mind to, and there's no doubt that I put more worry into every little detail of life than my dad or anyone else I've ever met, maybe even my grandma, but not a soul invests more strategy into life's projects than my father. And I'm proud to say that about him and to say that he's my dad.

For all the hard work we've invested together, especially his over the years, and for all the expectations I felt from him growing up that drove me never to settle for inferior with anything I did, even though less-than-perfect invariably happened sometimes, Dad also instilled a love of food in me. And that culinary adoration, particularly for cheeseburgers, has significantly shaped the man I've become. My grandmother and mother's cooking obviously showed me a world of creating in the kitchen that I didn't learn from anyone else. My mom's father absolutely relished food in a way that I've carried on. But my dad's understated love for simple meat-and-potatoes Southern cooking can't be missed when calculating why I am who I am.

Dad's a regular at Kim's Kitchen Family Restaurant in Stanley, North Carolina, our family's favorite place to eat over the years. The joint opened when I was a small boy and served the community for many years. After closing for several years, it reopened a few years back, and I can absolutely say without any doubt that no one was happier than Dad and me that Kim's returned to service. You see, they make the best cheeseburger in the world. I will forever defend that claim. I've often wanted to ask them for their recipe, but I've respected that they have such a good thing going, they can't be sharing out the family secrets to anyone, not even lifetime fanboys like me and Dad. Their burgers are all about the freshest, most tender and juicy burger meat, the meltiest cheese, the softest buns and how all of those ingredients work together in perfect harmony. I've eaten cheeseburgers across the country now through travels alone and with my wife, and no burger stacks up yet. Most don't even come close. And I have my father to thank for knowing that.

Through the years, I've never kept count of how many cheeseburgers we've eaten, at Kim's or anywhere, but the number's astronomically high. That's no understatement. And all those burgers might have produced health hazards our doctors wouldn't approve of, but they've been their own form of medicine, their own language even, that Dad and I have enjoyed. When we commune with cheeseburgers in hand, even simply at home with burgers my mom has made on the stovetop, time stands still a bit, anxieties relax, and we bond together with a common enjoyment of such a serene sandwich.

As much as I recall all the times I've devoured a burger alongside my father, I rarely remember him actually cooking one himself. He has the culinary prowess to make a burger, but Mom usually works the kitchen in their home, and she's quite good at it. (Just never ask her to make you something to eat with the reason that "she does it better" than you do. That's not a good reason, rather a clear indicator you just don't want to get up and do it for yourself. That's a warning not to levy that kind of reasoning on a food request for anybody, actually.) I do, however, remember a few times over the years when Dad has been in charge of making something, or when he's been the cook in the kitchen.

The first time that stands out in my mind is one of the great humorous moments in my life. One winter when I was a teenager and my mom was traveling in the northeastern U.S. with a friend, we received a heavy snowfall in the South that blanketed us for a few days. In need of simple meals while snowed in—as snowed in as you can be in the South, I suppose, though everything does close down more quickly when we get frozen precipitation down here—Dad set to unthawing frozen spaghetti in the microwave. That might not sound like much to you, but Mom's spaghetti and meatballs were very good for us not to have any Italian heritage in our bloodline. And they reheated quite well. Just remember, spaghetti cooks in water to begin with, so frozen spaghetti's deicing isn't really that unusual or awkward to a foodie with an open mind. Anyway, Dad was heating up the meal, when a "thwack" greeted us at the back sliding glass door off the den of our house. When we went to inspect the noise, we saw a bird had flown into the door, probably after seeing its reflection in the glass. That happened often at our house over the years. This time, the bird had dropped to the snowy deck below, and was sitting there dazed, staring into the glass. Dad paused from his work in the kitchen, walked over into the den, crawled into the floor and stuck his face right up to the glass. He was down on the bird's eye level, looking back at it. I don't remember what Dad said to the bird, but seeing him in the floor that day was about as goofy as my dad ever got. Maybe he had a little cabin fever from being snowed in. That kept him from getting outside and being productive as he liked to do. But that moment of humor between us—because we shared quite a few laughs over that dazed bird and Dad's approach—was so important. It showed a certain light side of my father that I now realize is an important reminder that we can't be so serious and hard on ourselves all the time.

    Dad is a good man, through and through. He taught me to work hard, but he used times like that bird's misfortunate crash to show me that fun and happiness are important, too. He wasn't normally silly, and neither was Grandpa, my mom's dad. The humorous take on life usually fell to the women in my family. But that day with that dang bird stands out as a time when Dad could be funny when the situation called for it. I've seen him laugh more and more as the years have gone by. It always gives me a boost when he finds something particularly funny, especially if it's something simple like that bird. I'd say my father appreciates smart humor, so it's noteworthy when he laughs at the simplicities of the world around us.

Simple's a good word to describe Dad's food tastes. A good cheeseburger sure can taste amazing, but it's just bread, meat and cheese no matter how you slice and stack it. That's by no means some fancy dish with rare ingredients like you see at chic, expensive restaurants. I think Dad's penchant for simple meat, potatoes, bread and cheese has significantly influenced my own tastes. When my wife Molly and I started our food blog #FoodieScore the first month we were married, we immediately developed its focus around simple culinary pleasures and conquests. We love sharing easy recipes and one-of-a-kind, home-cooking restaurants we visit, with the hopes that other people can discover and enjoy them, too. That's the kind of thing my dad has instilled in me over the years.

If I have to focus on one dish my dad's often made that reminds me of him, it will always be his Oyster Stew. Now, as a disclaimer, I'm actually not a huge fan of his stew. I never really have been, but I ate it as a child because I didn't want to displease him or offend him. My parents never expected me to clean my plate, but I always did no matter what was on it because I didn't want to waste food or come up short on doing my best at everything. Something inside me said that I had to eat everything in sight or else squander the opportunity. Bluntly, that led me to throw up quite a few times when I was a kid. There was one Thanksgiving when I polished off three massive plates of traditional favorites, which sent me to Grandma and Grandpa's bathroom to throw up. And there was the Christmas when I ate Oyster Stew quickly to get it down and then had to excuse myself to the restroom to throw up. I had a habit of eating fast and then involuntarily purging. I've always had a bad gag reflex, easily triggered by smells and flavors that are undesirable to my senses. Sounds can do it, too. That moment in the movie Four Christmases where Vince Vaughn sees the baby throw up and then says "I'm going to do it, too,"—yeah, that's me all the way.

I've always had a horrible ability to control feeling like I would throw up. Once, I puked in the cafeteria early in elementary school just at the sight of coleslaw. That set a precedent that I never had an appetite for a long time for lunch at school. So, I started balling up the sandwiches my mom would make me and throwing them away most days because I couldn't stomach them. I tossed them in the trash because I wanted her to think I was eating and didn't want to disappoint her that I wasn't. She took the time and money to prepare them, and I felt bad I didn't have the stomach for them. I'm sorry, Mom and Dad, but those actions taught me long ago that I shouldn't waste food at any cost. I could've just saved the sandwiches or told my parents that I couldn't eat. They would've had at least some suggestions to help me feel better about lunch, even if that meant carrying less food with me. Of course, in later years, I didn't want to eat lunch because I feared it would make me need to use the bathroom at school, which was always a panic-inducing thought.

So, I'm not a big Oyster Stew eater, but my Dad has long upheld the family tradition of making it on Christmas Eve every year. Some years because of extenuating circumstances, that annual rite of passage has moved to Christmas Day or another surrounding date, but mostly it's been on the Eve we celebrate Christ's birth. My grandparents enjoyed his stew very much, and my mom's dad even ate the oysters in the stew, something even my dad, the cook, doesn't do. He spends a couple hours working on the stew, and he's always his toughest critic on its quality when he's done. Gee, that sounds familiar. I like seeing him in the kitchen. I think it's always reminded me that anyone can cook when they want to, even if that's not their biggest gift or their favorite place to be. Dad's faithful to that Oyster Stew tradition, but while it has strengthened my connection with food as a form of fun and healing in a difficult world in which to live, his example of faith in God has been far more important.

Some of my most vivid memories over the years have been of my father reading devotions in the mornings, reading his Bible in the evenings and taking us to church on Sundays. On the outside, Dad's not the most forward Christian man you'll meet. He doesn't beat his chest and preach the Gospel to other people in public. He doesn't post Bible verses all over social media and share Sunday selfies of his #churchflow life either. But he always sticks with his reading and study of scriptures. I know he's a praying man, too. He's a God-fearing man, oh yes, to the point that he fears the wrath of God very much. I'm much like my dad in wondering in times of great struggle why God allows us to suffer on this earth before joining Him in Heaven. Though I really believe God allows us to face challenges in order to keep us close to Him and seeking Him, I can't help but wonder if I might incur God's wrath when I sin or fall short of properly crediting Him for all the blessings I receive and experience in my life. I think my dad wonders the same things, even though he's not fallen one bit short in guiding a Christian family. He's always encouraged my mom and me in reading the Bible, going to church and praying, most of all by doing it himself.

So, I guess my Dad is a "hard man." He's about as disciplined and set in his ways as you'll ever find, and I don't suggest you try to make him stray from that path. You'll find yourself in a battle you likely won't win without a Hall of Fame effort. But his determination and his hard work have absolutely gotten me somewhere. At my core, I appreciate what I have much more than I would have without his example. I also value my Bible and my spiritual relationship with my Savior, Jesus Christ, God in human form who I believe came to the earth to die and save us from our sins. I have complete faith in His truth, and I have Dad to thank for discovering it. That's enough right there for any father to bestow on his son. But in my case, there's also the matter of cheeseburgers. Boy, Dad, do I love a great cheeseburger, and I'm sure glad you do, too.

Oven Burger Sliders

There are many ways to make a burger, but I believe there are three qualities my dad would most require. One, you've got to use fresh hamburger meat. You can't use frozen or thawed meat for the best burger. Meat doesn't hold the same quality after freezing. I also believe 85-15 or higher is best because it is the leanest while providing just enough fat for flavor. Two, cheese is not negotiable. There is no such thing as a hamburger. You add cheese, and the meat and cheese become a sandwich as a cheeseburger. Three, you toast the bun lightly. I don't like a hard bun, and I don't like calling anything that houses a sandwich "crusty bread." I don't let sandwich shops toast my bun when they ask because they always overdo it for my taste. You want a light toasting.

My wife Molly found a perfect method for making a delicious cheeseburger with a slightly, perfectly toasted bun. There's a sauce that comes with it, which is really part of the original recipe, but I'm going to omit that for these purposes. Everyone has a favorite set of burger toppings. My mom loves just a little mayo and cheese. I love a good barbecue sauce and bacon combination. Dad prefers chili, mustard and onion, or as Kim's calls it, "all the way no slaw." You can add anything you like to these. The only requirement is to follow the cooking method.

What you need:
- At least 1 pound fresh hamburger meat
- 6-8 fresh buns (potato bread is a good hearty choice)
- Slices of cheese (You can choose which kind, but American melts perfectly with this method, and yes, I know there's plenty of debate about whether American is actually true cheese or just imitation cheese.)
- Salt
- Pepper
- Worcestershire sauce

What you do:
1. Place your ground meat in a bowl, shake in some salt, pepper and Worcestershire sauce, all for flavoring. It may take you several times of making this recipe to get it just how you like it. Mix it all together well.
2. Divide your meat into either 6 or 8 servings. Roll each into a ball. They don't have to be perfectly even. Use a hamburger press or your hands to flatten them into patties. If you use a press, you'll need a couple sheets of parchment paper to keep the meat from sticking to the press.
3. Next, cook your hamburger patties. You can use any method you like, including the stovetop on medium heat, the grill over an open flame, or our favorite, in the oven. We've found that the oven on about 375 degrees cooks hamburger meat evenly without getting it too brown outside, about 20 minutes, and a lot of fat drips out while the patties maintain a delightful juiciness. We're not sure how it does all that at once, but there's some kind of magic involved. We just cover a baking sheet with foil, add our patties, cover it with the foil and stick it in the oven.
4. If you've cooked your meat in the oven, leave it on for coming steps. If not, go ahead and preheat it to 350.
5. Drain the burger patties. As a trick, I like to use a saved aluminum can, the type you get from canned vegetables or meat, to pour my grease into. It solidifies eventually if you sit it behind the sink a while, and you can throw it away without any mess.
6. Take each bun and top it with a patty. Then add a slice of cheese to each and affix the top half of the bun. You can add toppings you want to heat at this point, but you don't have to. That can still come later.
7. Take each individual burger and wrap it in a small piece of foil.
8. Load all of your wrapped burgers onto a baking sheet and put

the tray in the oven.
9. Bake them for 12 to 15 minutes. You don't have to worry too much about the timing because your meat is already cooked.
10. When you take your burgers out of the oven, the cheese will be melted all over the beef, and your buns will have a slight toastiness to them. You can still add toppings, or you can eat them basic as the bun-meat-cheese combo. Either way, we love these oven burgers, and we like making them as sliders because the smaller size helps us justify eating a couple!

THE PRISON OF MY OWN BRAIN

I have a habit of using metaphors to compare perspectives in my life. I'll let you decide whether my penchant for these metaphors is a good or bad trait. The broad entity of sports has been one of the most common comparison grounds for me. Food has been the other most often-used basis of comparison for experiences in my life, and one of my former newspaper executives gave me an analogy that I've used and imparted often. He first laid it on my brain as a suggestion for how I should approach difficult conversations with subordinates—particularly for use when dealing with an employee he didn't really work with well.

I'll eliminate the unnecessary four-letter words he inserted into his management metaphor, but it doesn't change any of the meaning. He basically compared his preferred approach to providing tough feedback as serving a sandwich. You start with good news and end with good news, and you sandwich those layers with the bad news in the middle. Therefore, he said, you're giving someone a s*** sandwich. Not very appetizing, but that's the route he discussed taking. So, I tried it, and I learned that I didn't much like how it felt, imparting concerns that way. It felt much better just being honest from the start, but trying to also highlight things an employee did well. No matter how you slice it, middle management jobs are difficult, and giving feedback to a struggling employee "below" you at the demand of a boss "above" you is also tough. You're really caught in between. Essentially, you become the bad news—all the time. I took quite a bit of pain and anxiety from my years in middle management in the journalism world.

As much as I came to dread the "sandwich" talk, it's exactly what I'm serving up to you right now. I'll be honest and tell you that. Smack dab in the middle of fond memories of the family members in my life who have given me so much of themselves to create the person I am, for better and for worse, there's been a whole lot of torture and agony in my own life that sits right in the middle of where I've been and who I am. So much time in my life has come in the presence of no one, and that's just how I've often wanted things to be. Alone time is very important to me as an opportunity to reset my brain, to write and to think to help me understand how I feel and what I need. But being by myself has also created many opportunities to torture and hurt myself.

So, this section of this story will be quite difficult to read. Believe me, it's no less difficult to admit and write. It's where I'll divulge some of my most exhausting and self-wounding experiences I've undergone with no one else present. It's literally the s*** right in the middle of this food-and-fear account of my anxiety-filled life. And it's quite possibly the most important passage for people to read in this whole book. I need you to understand just how bad parts of my life have been inside the prison of my own brain. And I want you to take from these memories and admissions just how bad some of my decisions have been. Then I beg you to not repeat my mistakes. I have also come to plead with myself to avoid making these errors again. While these times in my life have also included great blessings—food, faith and family joys included—there have been vast dark moments when living has been arduous, warlike and even, at times, in question.

SELF-TORTURE: PART ONE

I've already told you about my elementary school bathroom nightmare, so I'll try not to recap too much. Those events have had a profoundly negative impact on my life. I wonder greatly where those boys are now in their lives. Are they happy? Do they even have a fleeting recollection of that day in that restroom? Do they remember who I am the way I recall their first and last names, their faces, what they were wearing, and just how frightened public restrooms make me to this day? I still dread walking into a men's bathroom, especially if I need to sit down. Many men's stalls do not lock. Toilets are incredibly dirty. Men curse and joke around and horseplay in bathrooms at all ages. These are not places I like to be. Bad memories return often, and the fact of life that I need to empty waste in public creates a sense of panic when I go almost anywhere.

There's at least one part of that whole experience that has improved, however, at least most of the time. I no longer spend hours each morning damaging my body to keep such restroom visits from being necessary. It's taken me years of my life to change my bad habits, though, and I'm still dealing with physical damage from what I've done in my past. This takes incredible courage to say, so I hope you'll understand its importance and the fragility I feel in honestly sharing it. When I was in elementary school, continuing into middle and high school, and even during my adult years at times, I've spent multiple hours on the toilet each morning, straining with all my might to get every drop of waste out of my body in the hopes that I won't need to visit a restroom again to sit down until I return to the safety of my own home. That all started after that nightmare in the school bathroom.

I remember quite a few days in the middle of my grade-school career that I would rise before five-thirty in the morning, go through a very obsessive, self-created schedule of going to the bathroom at least four times, taking a quick shower, eating a very specific light breakfast, sitting in a recliner in my parents' living room and pushing my body as hard as possible on the toilet every morning, trying to keep myself from being embarrassed again. I never forgot, and still haven't, what it felt like to be humiliated that day in third grade in the bathroom. I felt so exposed. A lot of people dream about being on a toilet with their pants down in public. I've lived that nightmare. And it wasn't just that one time.

There was a visit to a retail superstore as a child, I don't remember my exact age, where two boys peeked over and under my stall, pointed and laughed at me. I believe that was well before my school debacle, so I was already wounded when that time came. I just remember being very upset when I returned to my mom in that store. That wasn't the only other time my stomach's natural human needs impacted me with feelings of shame.

In sixth grade, I once needed to use the bathroom during my after-lunch reading class. No way was I going to go to the bathroom in the fear that someone would point, laugh and spread embarrassment for me. So I held it—as I decided I'd always do in school. My stomach started making all kinds of growling and gurgling sounds. Two girls were sitting across from me at my reading table. They started giggling. They kept giggling. Other people in the room started listening. My stomach gurgled louder and growled louder until the class period ended. I couldn't escape until the school bell told me I was allowed. I'll never forget those girls' faces. I'm sure they've forgotten mine by now. Sadly, that's how life goes. Those of us who hold on to specific pains never forget. Everyone else is able to let go because they have no reason to remember. The tormenter moves on. The tormented soul never does.

That day in sixth grade really cemented the concerns that had plagued me since that incident in the third-grade boys bathroom. After the stomach-noise situation, I really doubled over and doubled down on my straining efforts in the bathroom each morning. There were times when I'd sit on the toilet for up to two hours at a time, going through a systematic number of pushes in which I attempted to empty my bowels as much as possible. Usually, I pushed myself in sequences of eights, which I believe I set as a guideline because of an obsessive thought that my work in those numbers would correlate to the eight hours I hoped to make it each day without needing to use the restroom again. If I left the house after seven something in the morning, eight hours later would carry me until after three, and that would likely mean I would already be home, or at least not in a quiet classroom surrounded by other potentially mean-spirited people.

My bathroom routine was really where I developed a lot of compulsive habits—and I have no doubt that I have Obsessive-Compulsive Disorder that has stemmed from those activities. The number three has become one of my most hated of all digits, and it's quite the silly reason why that's the case. I experienced so many stomach aches as a child and dealt with so much diarrhea that I came to associate a number with what felt, to me, like a combination of going "number one" and "number two." If number one was urinating and number two was defecating, then "number three" was a diarrhea-like combination of numbers one and two. I don't remember when I first made that up, but it became a standard by which I always hated the number three in all applications. So, eight was a good number, the hours I hoped to safely navigate the day without the need to sit in a bathroom in public. And three was a horrible number, associated with the consistency of material in my stomach that I dreaded most.

Most mornings, when I got into the bathroom, I actually had "business" to attend to just two or three times. The other visits to the restroom were attempts at pushing out anything remaining in my system that might become a problem during the school day. Occasionally, I'd strain so hard on the toilet that I'd push stomach acid out into the toilet. I know this because of the sound it made, and I know this because of the clear color that would appear on the toilet paper. I know that's graphic, but it's important to relate to show you how far I pushed myself because of fear.

Usually, I'd grip the wall with my left hand and the toilet paper holder with my right hand, for leverage that would help me to push as hard as possible. If I felt a grinding feeling in my backside, I knew

I was getting a good push. It was very difficult if nothing happened. That made me feel like I was failing and doomed to need a bathroom that day, so I'd just push that much harder. Sometimes I'd strain so forcefully that I would feel a little lightheaded. I could feel my pulse pounding in my temples. My eyes would dim a bit, like my vision was suffering. Blood would squirt into the toilet.

Suffering was exactly what I was doing, in the names of bullying, embarrassment, fear and outright anxiety. My whole routine made absolutely no sense whatsoever. Why would the counting of strains matter? How could such reasoning and self-torture actually help me? Well, I now know the truth is that it didn't do anything but "kick the can down the road" on all my problems. But when you're fearful and full of anxiety, you don't think straight. That's what I want you to understand. People do a lot of horrible things when their mental health is poor. Many hurt others. I hurt myself. And hurt myself, wow, I sure did.

My backside has been a source of pain often for me over the years. I basically gave myself teenage hemorrhoids from all my straining. I used a combination of petroleum jelly, hemorrhoid pads and other devices to try to heal myself as much as I could each night. Then, I'd go right back to straining the next morning. It was a vicious cycle of pain. My body hurt bad, but my mind was in the worst shape of all. I remember one day in eighth grade when I had pushed myself so forcefully that morning that I had rubbed myself raw on my bottom. I had an algebra test that day, and I knew the class would be quiet. If I needed to go to the bathroom, everyone would know it because my stomach would be noisy. So, I erroneously thought I could push everything out and eliminate such a problem. I damaged my bottom so badly that I had to squirm in my seat all through that class and that test. I freaked out at the thought of not finishing it and getting a bad grade. Math was always difficult for me, even though teachers thought I was very good at it. Numbers have never been my thing, other than basic arithmetic, which I'm very skilled with, especially statistics due to my love for sports and the numbers of the games. Words are more my thing. So, any kind of math adversity really took shots at my anxiety. And I always seemed to have math classes late in the day, which made my concerns about silent test periods that much worse.

In the mornings, it was my concern that eating such a light breakfast—always half a piece of mom's homemade banana bread and a quarter of a small mug or cup of milk—would not be enough to keep my stomach from growling due to hunger. In the afternoons, it most worried me that my little bit of breakfast, any lunch I ate and any failure at going to the bathroom correctly that morning would lead to me needing to use the bathroom. I taught myself to always hold any urges until I could get home. I imagine I pushed so much back inside me that it was very bad for my stomach and all other parts of my gastrointestinal tract. That activity is probably why I've continued to experience upset stomachs as an adult. Grownups are really no better at being understanding to people with stomach issues than kids. In some cases, they're much worse.

I once sat in an office meeting with a few Christian adults who joked about Irritable Bowel Syndrome, making fun of a company with the initials IBS and finding humor in a previous coworker who had the issue. They had no idea, to my knowledge, that they were in the presence of a guy who'd dealt with IBS all his life and hid it because people make fun of it, a man who associates quite a bit of pain with such things. So, they kept laughing, and inside I just wanted to cry. But like my bathroom needs, I held it in.

As I took office jobs and career positions that forced me to deal constantly with people, I continued to experience deep fear over needing to use the bathroom around others. So many mornings, I held onto my bathroom routine, even after I had grown and finished school. I didn't necessarily strain for quite as long, but I'd still visit the restroom a specific number of times each morning and push myself in groups of eight, still thinking that making it that many hours would be a success. Sadly, I continued to fail, still needing, many days, to go to the bathroom, and having to hold it when I couldn't. Many years after I first experienced that pain in the elementary toilet stall, I realized that I suffer from a truly nervous stomach. When I'm upset about anything, I find I more often need to go to the bathroom. And when I need to go to the bathroom, I get more fearful and feel deep anxiety. The two go hand in hand, the mental illness and the physical illness. It's a constant battle for me, one that I'll likely fight all my life. If I have to take a positive from it, it's that I've now learned and understand where I've been in that fight in my past and how I must adapt for my future. Through all that straining, I've hurt myself in many ways. Now, I must keep striving to minimize my tendency to think that pushing my body will keep me from further embarrassment. That makes no sense. It's a typical human need to expel waste. I must remember that. I wish toilet humor wasn't so prized in America. I just don't understand it. I guess that's because my experience with toilets has been vastly different than most other people's.

You might think after reading all of these accounts: How in the world can you talk about this kind of stuff in a book that also includes discussion about food and recipes? Well, that's the twisted irony of my life and the world. It's who I am, this weird combination of experiences. During this particular part of my life, the teenage years, and during other periods, I didn't much enjoy food. Most of my meals were carefully calculated in an effort to prevent more nightmares in the presence of other people. For example, I particularly loved the chicken strips and corn on the cob at a restaurant where my family often ate lunch after church on Sundays. But I learned as a young man that my digestive system struggles to process corn. If I ate corn on Sunday, it wouldn't give me stomach issues until Monday, while I was at school. So, I had to stop eating it and just order fries. Food and fear have always been intimately linked in my life. That truth is a major part of my story.

SELF-TORTURE: PART TWO

When most people think of mental illness and harm, one of two things come to mind: either that person has a tendency to hurt other people or to do something to themselves that either involves an activity like "cutting" or the ultimate damage, suicide. Neither of those have applied to me, so I think it's important to share my viewpoint and where I've been in this part of the mental illness fight. I've never considered cutting myself, and I've always tried very intensely to not hurt anyone else. I won't say that my actions and words have never damaged other people, because I believe many of us say and do things that cause pain to others, even sometimes unintentionally, but I've never intentionally set out to harm or abuse anyone, including physically. And I have a serious disrespect for others who attempt knowing damage.

When I've been frustrated or upset, especially with myself, I've had a tendency to hit myself. Sometimes, it's just been a slap of the knee. Other times, I've punched myself in the gut. Occasionally, I've slammed myself in the head. No matter which, they've all been wrong choices. Taking frustration out by hurting my body doesn't help anything. I believe it disappoints God, too, because harming myself is taking a swing at His creation. He made me, and I know He doesn't want me to destroy anything He's made. Self-torture has been one of my worst approaches to life with anxiety and depression. It's another piece of that erroneous thought process that develops when you aren't thinking clearly.

I'm sure plenty of people have lightly smacked themselves out of frustration, clapping their hands, slapping their leg or doing something similar out of irritation. But to actually take a swing at themselves? That's not normal. However, it has been for me. There have been many times when I've pounded on my arms or legs or chest, or even my head, in anger, usually about myself and my own life, but occasionally out of irritation that other people have made my life more difficult.

Taking shots at my head with the back of my hand or with my fist has been my worst set of choices. It seems incredibly ridiculous, but I've done it on many occasions. And in later years I've come to wonder if I might have concussion-type symptoms later in life due to damage to my brain. All the talk about football injuries and collisions has just further made me worry about that possibility. Have I hurt myself internally by punching and prodding myself? Maybe, and I might find out down the road as I age more.

Let me just say that there's absolutely no sense in the world in hitting yourself. I wouldn't dream of putting a hand on someone else, but so often I've laid hands on myself, and I don't mean in the positive religious sense. I'm certain that makes me considerate of other people in some way, while also making me sound crazy. Who hits themselves? Well, I have plenty of times, for some reason choosing to not point the finger at other people and in lieu turn it around and point it at myself, whether it's my fault or not. In times when I feel I've failed, I've hit myself. When others have hurt me and I've been mad, I've hit myself. When it's been a combination of me and other people being wrong, I've hit myself. No matter the cause, hitting myself has been a standard activity in my life, and that's been a very wrong approach. It's taken me doing it in front of my wife for me to see how silly it seems and how bad it's been for my health—and the health of other people I love.

I won't say that I don't hit myself anymore. From time to time, I either do it out of habit or I lose my cool a little more and a pound on my knee or chest slips. But I've done far less of it in recent months and years. Now, I'm more likely to try to quickly remind myself when the feeling rises to just let go of the moment of anger. That's very difficult to do, so I've had to develop strategies to keep myself from resorting to pounding on my body. One of the best techniques has been to talk to God. It helps me to just tell God that I'm mad, disappointed, upset, frustrated or anxious. Sometimes I tell my wife or my mom that I feel my anxiety starting to peak. That helps, too, as a means of just unloading my feelings verbally instead of channeling them through my hands and then hitting them back into my body. We do a lot of things when we have a mental illness or mental health problem, and much of it makes no sense. While most people think those of us with such challenges just harm others, it's not that uncommon that we only hurt ourselves.

I'm very blessed that God has kept me from harming myself further. I've never felt a desire to cut my wrists or shoot myself or anything that severe. But what I've done with my fists has been bad enough. Does that make me crazy, turning my hands on my own body? In some ways I believe it does. But I am glad to say that I have learned that it doesn't solve anything. I never felt better after pounding on myself. I quite literally just added to my pain. Now, when I tell God that I'm upset or troubled, I actually feel a lightening of my frustration. It's like sending my irritation into the air to float away and die. The new approach helps quite a bit to lessen my anxiety instead of causing harm that keeps the cycle going.

SELF-TORTURE: PART THREE

As much as I tried to keep myself from food at earlier times in my life to avoid stomach issues, I switched to a different gear altogether after college, when I moved out on my own and lived alone for about eight years before I married. During that time, food became a major vice by which I harmed myself. Every stressor and bully that impacted me at work and in the world in general led me to damage my body with more food. Eating became my vice by which I would take out all my anxiety about my life. Naturally, that led to more stomach problems, more toilet trouble and weight gain that left me in a very unhealthy condition.

Life in the news business is incredibly stressful. I love hearing and telling people's stories, and I've always been told I'm good with people and good at writing, so those details make it sensible why I would go into journalism. Sports have always been a passion of mine, so I combined that with writing and people to create a dream career of sports journalism. I didn't stick with the sports part for very long though, deciding at an early age that working nights and weekends didn't appeal to me. It's ironic that just a year and a half into my news career I was promoted and switched to working nights and weekends, with very little sports coverage involved. Living on a schedule of getting up around noon and going to bed about three in the morning, combined with long periods of not eating and intense periods of packing in a lot of food, had a very negative impact on my body and my mind. I gained a lot of weight in the first several years after college—and that continued for quite a while, until I met my wife and decided I needed to make significant changes or risk dying early.

When I lived on my own those first few years after college, I ate anything and everything I could get my hands on after work, especially once I started working night shifts. After I'd leave work at ten or eleven in the evening, I'd either visit a fast food restaurant or go home and pack as much into my body as possible, trying to cover up the stress of the day. I really didn't think through the whole journalism thing correctly. I had made my career choice without considering how it would further my worrisome nature. I made a lot of decisions in my younger years with a hurried feeling, like I could never pause a second to think deeply, because thinking deeply always felt to me like an opportunity to slip into an anxiety-riddled spiral of fear.

When you work in news, someone's always going to be unhappy with you, but with anxiety, I wanted to keep everyone happy all the time. I wasn't happy with myself, so I couldn't handle others being upset with me. That didn't mesh well with journalism. No matter what story I wrote, edited or headlined, someone would complain. That's just the nature of the business, and that's only become truer in the insatiable era of the 24-hour Internet news cycle. Journalism is a career in which it's impossible to make everyone—editors, publishers, advertisers, readers, fellow reporters—happy. So, it produced a ton of anxiety in me, but I didn't know that's what I should call it. I just thought I was always stressed. I was, but it was more than that. On days off work, I'd often stay in bed much of the day, only getting up to eat large amounts of food. I stuck to myself most of the time, not really making a lot of friends. That didn't really help me make contacts, which is the life blood for working in journalism. It's all about who you know, and the more people you know, the more stories you help break.

Instead of hobnobbing with people in the community, I'd stay at home and eat and wallow in my sadness from any adversity I faced the previous week and might face the following week. Food became a gigantic torture device for all of that pain. As I said before, I once ate more than a hundred shrimp in a food challenge at a local sports bar. Another time I polished off a whole five-dollar pizza from a chain restaurant, a bad decision that left me hurting the next morning with indigestion that I mistakenly thought might be a heart attack. I called my mother fearing the worst, and I called out of work that day, thinking I might actually be dying. Well, I was killing myself, but I didn't realize how. Other times, I fell asleep with rib bones on my chest after eating a whole rack and a pile of hushpuppies following a particularly eventful and stressful week in the office. Around that same time, I recall demolishing two boxes of oatmeal cream pies in one sitting. I opened one after another from their plastic wrappings and stuffed them in my mouth, basically swallowing them whole. My mouth was sore after such exercises.

I gained a lot of weight during the period in time that I lived by myself and worked in news, which was the largest portion of my adult life so far. But I think the physical torture I commenced with food wasn't nearly as damaging as the mental torture cycle I created for myself. Looking back, I shouldn't have chosen such a stressful career to begin with. Because I didn't understand that I suffered from true mental illnesses—anxiety and depression—for so long, I didn't realize that I should've researched careers that meshed better with those conditions. I just chose a field that I could do and succeed in. That lack of deep investigation led to eventually leaving journalism and moving into public relations, which became a marketing job and stressed me out further, and that led to me leaving that career as well. Young people, please learn from my mistakes, strive to better understand your own mind, and select a career that will pair well with your unique life challenges.

Instead of taking care of myself and being kind in a way that would enable me to have a rewarding career while battling my mental obstacles, I set myself up with jobs that taxed my mind and led me to attempt to bury my fears in food. That was absolutely the worst thing I could have done, especially considering all the stomach problems I already faced. When I started eating to hide my insecurities, my weight increased and so did all my stomach issues. I started going to the bathroom more than ten times each day on average, because of all the bad food I was eating. There was a day I remember clearly in which I stopped at a chain fast food restaurant on the way to my afternoon shift at a newspaper. Like it was yesterday, I easily recall ordering two cheeseburgers, two chicken sandwiches, two large orders of fries and a large sweet tea. I ate all of it in about five minutes and then drove to the office for my shift. I felt badly the whole day, had to visit the bathroom repeatedly, which worried me every time, then went home alone and fell asleep that night. Binging and then not eating the rest of the day is a very bad cycle to repeat, and it's exactly what I'd do most of the time. When I became an editor in journalism, I'd often sit in my chair for hours at a time without moving, just staring at my screen and constantly looking at words. It was a combination of a sedentary lifestyle and a bad diet that really attacked my health, and it's caused me to have to work harder years later to fix all the problems I've experienced as a result.

People utilize a number of vices in the world to try to deal with pain. Some seek drugs or alcohol as their vices. Mine has often been food and large quantities of it. I've done a lot of harm to myself with something that I should have enjoyed. Food has always been an important part of my family and the traditions of life in the American South. When I started using it to harm my body, I put my life in danger. I had to change my ways of eating and thinking about food to reverse the damage. And it took me a long time to understand that, just as long as it took me to understand I had anxiety in the first place.

So, for much of my life, I've been in the dark both about how deep my anxiety has been and about sharing most of my deepest, darkest secrets with other people. I've chosen many times to battle my struggles alone, save for consulting God effectively at times and ineffectively in others. I say ineffectively because hitting myself and then asking for forgiveness over and over again doesn't make much sense. There's no real healing that happens using that method. Real healing begins when I ask God to forgive me and help me not to hit myself at all. Real healing begins when I stop straining on the toilet and start sitting down only when I need to actually use the bathroom. Real healing begins when I start eating for my health and to purely enjoy food.

As much as this section has been difficult to write and just as torturous to read, there have been positives that have come from the times in my life when I've spent many hours alone. Living as a bachelor has helped me develop creative, unique ways of cooking certain meals that can be useful for individuals and for families. My experiences cooking for just one person have certainly carried over to married life. Many of them have found their way to the food blog, #FoodieScore, that my wife and I publish online. And I am pleased to share a few of my simplest recipes with you here.

Simple Chicken-Cheese Quesadillas

When I lived by myself for about eight years before marrying my wife, I cooked a lot but tried my best to keep dirty dishes at a minimum. As I've learned to bake and developed a love for it, I've had to relinquish my hopes to keep the kitchen sink free of dirty plates, pans, glasses and measuring cups. But in the past, I came up with a number of simple dishes that didn't really require recipes, measuring or much cleanup. I like to think of those meals as "Improv Cooking," something that appeals to my creative yet simplistic nature. One of my favorite such creations was always this prescription for quesadillas, and it's a "recipe," if you can even call it that, that my wife and I still occasionally enjoy today, even as I have grown more skilled and confident in cooking and baking. This is a very cheap, easy meal, and I think it's even one you can help use to teach kids some basics in the kitchen with adult supervision. It's also a cheap, filling and satisfying option for poor college students with little kitchen access in a residence hall.

What you need:
- 1 can white meat chicken (right off the shelf)
- 1 pack flour tortillas (any size, but medium is best)
- 1 bag shredded cheese (you won't use it all)
- Butter for grilling

What you do:
1. Start by draining your chicken. I like to use a can opener around the edge, just until there's a slight bit of the seal remaining. That way I can use the lid to help drain the juices into the sink.
2. Now, place a few tortillas, as many as you want to make into quesadillas, onto a clean counter or cutting board.
3. Take the chicken in your hands and shred it onto half of each tortilla, where it is thinly and evenly distributed.
4. Top the chicken halves with shredded cheese, enough to really cover the chicken well.

5. Fold over the empty half of each tortilla.
6. Melt your butter in a frying pan on medium heat, turning the pan to distribute the butter as evenly as possible on the surface.
7. Once your pan is greased and heated, add one tortilla to the pan. Allow it to brown on one side before turning it to brown the other side. Turn it with the closed side completely against the pan so that the ingredients do not fall out.
8. Repeat this process until all of your quesadillas are heated and browned. I've always loved how melty inside and slightly crispy outside these quesadillas are when done. If you want to further simplify the process and you have a toaster oven, you can even toast each quesadilla in there for simpler cleanup!

Pizza Puffs (aka Savory Italian Monkey Bread)

Of all the classes in all my grade school years, I remember my Home Economics course as well as any other. What does that tell you about the kind of man I am? Hey, my wife calls me a domestic delight, so I guess I picked up a few skills that are useful! My middle school home-ec teacher taught us how to sew pillows, bake easy homemade chocolate chip cookies and make this very simple dinner called Pizza Puffs. This is another recipe I liked making years later when I lived on my own because it was cheap, required no measuring or recipe haggling, and I often ate the dinner right out of the baking pan. You can do that when you live alone! Who's going to complain? It's amazing that I learned how to bake this dish as I was going through some incredibly painful mental and physical health challenges smack dab in the heart of my two years of middle school. Somehow, this memory survived as a positive moment among all the difficulty.

What you need:
- 1 can of 8 refrigerated biscuits
- Your favorite jarred pizza sauce
- Shredded cheese
- Cooking spray
- Any other desired toppings

What you do:
1. Cut your biscuits into four pieces each.
2. Line the bottom of a sprayed/greased 8-by-8 pan with all your biscuit pieces.
3. Cover with your desired amount of pizza sauce.
4. Add any other toppings you'd like, such as pepperoni.
5. Cover the whole dish with cheese.
6. Bake in a 375-degree oven for 15 to 20 minutes, depending on how your oven heats and how brown you want the topping.
7. This recipe serves 2 to 4 people, depending on your eaters and how hungry they are.

SIGNS OF STRUGGLE AND SUPPORT

Many people claim they have the greatest mother in all the world. I won't say all those people are wrong. I will just vehemently argue that my mother is actually the greatest in all the world. If she qualified on all terms, I believe my mother would meet the standards for sainthood. That's not meant to be a sacrilegious statement. It's just that my mother is so great, so selfless and so lovingly thoughtful that I can't help but deeply appreciate her, even as I know I have never appreciated her enough and can never repay her for how much love she has given me all my life.

I am certain that my mother has served as a conduit of sorts for the anxiety that found its way into my genes and into every stage of my life. She is the link between me and the grandmother whose worrisome tendencies I have now assumed, also carrying many of those weighty burdens of fear and depressed thoughts. Like Grandma and me, Mom has traveled through the depths of a despair-filled mind. She has experienced sadness all by herself and struggled with her mental health for much of her life. Stomach trouble has plagued many of her days, just like Grandma and just like me. All of these things are connections of at least three generations in my family. But so is kindness and care and compassion, food and family and faith.

Mom has stuck with God throughout her life, and for that

example of faith through fear and tremendous adversity, I am exceedingly grateful. She has also stuck with me, never giving up on me and never saying "Son, I'm through with you and all this difficulty in your life. I can't take any more." I know there have been days, like there are for all mothers and all fathers and all people, when she's wanted to toss me aside, throw up her hands and scream, "Enough!" How could that not be a temptation? But she never has. Instead, she has faithfully stuck by my side every single day of my life. If she could do it, she did it, for me and for our family and for God. And my, what an example of care and compassion and consistency she is. Quite literally, she is a machine, always serving God by serving others instead of just serving herself. Even when she has been weary from anxiety of her own, depression of her own, stomach pain of her own, she has continued to be a daughter, wife, mother and child of God above all. If I can be half the person my mother is, to borrow from the similar and very familiar phrase, then I'll be all right.

My mother has always been there for me and with me, through everything from the very beginning. That's what mothers do, at least the good ones who accept and carry out the duty God assigned when He created mothers in the first place. They give us life. They prepare us for life. They continue to guide us through life. When they leave us and depart this life, they continue to impact our life through what they did in theirs. Mothers are eternal, much like God is eternal. There's a great burden on mothers to care for and love their children. What an incredible responsibility, but also what an amazing blessing and opportunity. My mother has been and seen and done and battled and remained steadfast in all these things. My mama is the greatest.

Mom's ability to craft delicious food is—as this book has progressed with each part of the story—a major part of my life. And it's a skill she has passed along to me, along with, I'm afraid, the tendencies to worry and feel guilt and experience depression. Mama's cooking has shaped my life and my enjoyment of being in the kitchen perhaps more than anyone else's. But before I step into our relationship in the kitchen, I want to go right back to the other room in the house where so much of my anxiety has resided, and that's the bathroom.

She isn't proud of it, but my mother is the one who imparted on me the understanding that everything in our bodies is eternally connected. When we have issues in our nose and throat at the same time, it's because the parts are linked. When our head aches and our eyes hurt, it's because the parts are linked. And when we're worried incessantly about something and our stomach bothers us, it's because the parts are linked. Everything in our body is associated with all the other parts of our bodies. Mom taught me so many things, and she's the one whose lessons about worry and stomach problems finally permeated my brain after all these years. All those things she kept telling me as a child and a teenager and an adult finally started to make sense and stick when I reached my thirties. I'm blessed that they finally joined, like the pieces of a puzzle that took a long time to solve.

Everything my mother has taught me has come with a backdrop of family and faith. She's been allegiant to both throughout her life, even when enemies and friends alike have attempted to make that difficult or impossible. She has not given up, and I have her most of all to thank for my not giving up, even when I haven't wanted to exist anymore. Eventually, my stomach problems and embarrassments and bullies weighed so heavily on me, that I sunk into a deep bout of depression from time to time that had me saying every morning, "I'm so tired, I don't want to do this anymore. I don't want to live, God. You can take me when you're ready. If it's my time, I'm ready to leave this earth."

But I never gave up, and I never stopped seeing scripture in my head. And that's because my mother never stopped putting scripture in front of me. All those times that I visited the bathroom over and over every morning, I'd emerge and walk toward the car to ride or drive to school and a Bible verse would be waiting for me on a little sticky-backed slip of paper. She'd leave them on the table and on my backpack to find before she drove me to school. When I started driving myself in my sophomore year of high school, she'd pen a verse and place it on my steering wheel when she'd crank my car. She knew I'd be sitting in the bathroom stressing about the whole day every morning. She prayed for me. She left that verse. She stuck with me all day and was waiting at home for me every night. Mom was always there, and she made sure God was always there, too. Yes, she and Dad took me to church on Sundays for Sunday school and services, and on Sunday nights for youth group, and on other days for other fellowship and service events, but it was her faithfulness to God and to His word and to me at home that changed my world and eventually changed my life. Mom ministered to me through continuously reading the Bible and sharing that with me, every day of the week, not just on Sundays.

A major part of why I believe God created everything, including me, and loves everyone, including me, and saved everyone, including me, by coming to earth and being a man named Jesus and dying on the cross to save me from my sins and rising into Heaven and being in charge of all that is and will be…is my Mom. She brought me into this world, and she did not leave me in it alone. Isn't that, by itself, a reason to celebrate a mother as spectacular? When she passes away, she will not ever leave me in it alone. Her lessons and her love will always be with me. And they have helped sustain me through all the deep dark passages I have navigated in all my years. My mom is an all-time great, a saint, a true Christian woman whose examples continue to amaze me.

When I grew up and moved out of the house, Mom didn't stop sharing the Word of God with me. She's emailed me devotions and Bible verses, and now that I'm married she continues to text me and my wife a Bible verse every single weekday morning as encouragement that we can and will make it through the day with God's ever-present and never-failing love and support. As much as she's faithful in reading the scriptures herself, she's just as faithful in sharing them with me and my wife. You can set your alarm clock by her early morning verses. If we added a loud tone on our smartphones to her text messages, it would wake us every weekday morning, usually before seven. She is a machine with her faithfulness to God and her children.

There have been so many times when I have not appropriately appreciated my mother, and I am incredibly ashamed to tell you that. I have fought with her and argued with her and been rude to her and made her feel unwanted and unsuccessful in her parenting more times than I could possibly count. I feel great guilt for that, but I believe deep down I have also expressed my gratitude enough times that she knows I love her and cannot live without her spirit. Of all things, in my darkest adult days of depression, there have been times when I didn't understand why she thought Bible verses would help me deal with my anxiety and depression. At those moments, I was blinded by my poor mental health, one of many ways mental illnesses blind me and can blind any person they encroach upon. I was so far down the hole of fear and grief that I couldn't see the light at the surface. She was that light. God's Word was that light. Thank you, Mom, for remaining faithful and shining.

Mom has seen me at my very worst for years, and she has never given up on me. A few years ago, my mother gave me an incredible gift on my thirty-second birthday. Before I was even born, when she had just learned she was pregnant with me and would be having a child, she started keeping a journal of entries written directly to me. At first, she called me Baby. When I was born and they named me Matthew, my name became the address of each entry. Just like everything else in her parenting and her life, she was faithful for years to always write to me, perhaps skipping days and even weeks or months here or there as she was busy attending to family responsibilities and desires, but always returning to the journal to write to me again. This book will be invaluable should my wife and I ever bring our own children into the world. It's like a parenting manual, a real-life guide to how the previous generation in my family that raised me handled wide-ranging situations, both good and bad. But it's already been so valuable in other ways. For one, it's reminded me just how a mother should love her child, with uncompromising, unceasing and unconditional care and compassion, just as God loves all His children. But it's also revealed to me just how much my mother has noted my anxiety throughout my entire life. I believe she's known for a long time that I've suffered from anxiety and depression, just by watching me and how I've approached life. However, those observations aren't something I believe can just be translated or imparted on another person. My own understanding of my mental health can't be transferred from my mother's brain. I had to come to understand what I'd been dealing with myself. Mom's book has been an incredible resource, dating back more than thirty years, for helping me navigate and grasp my mind and its up-and-down journey.

"Dear Matthew," as the journal is titled, dates to 1984, the year I came into the world. It's a powerful reminder of what a mother's love should be, and of the roller coaster ride parenting will always be, no matter what a family faces. There have been innumerable advantages I've received in my life, all from God and my parents, and there have been incredible challenges I've faced. But at the end of the day, this journal has reminded me who I am, where I come from, and how I should see the world and treat other people. The journal is a reminder that my mother has been with me for the whole journey, and the book itself has helped open my eyes to understand that my anxiety is a mental illness, not just a passing worry. Anxiety and depression and Obsessive-Compulsive Disorder and all of these illnesses I live with are part of who I am. I can't change them or drop them on command, but I can live with them, manage them, learn to love and not hate myself, and find ways to thrive despite having them as part of my life. "Dear Matthew" was an important piece in discovering and admitting just how impacted by mental illness my life has been, and it's led me to share my journey with others, in the hope that I can spread awareness and compassion among other people who battle similar challenges, either in their own minds or in the brains and lives of others they know and love.

With my mother's permission, here are a few of the most-revealing entries from "Dear Matthew" that provided perspective for me to understand that my anxiousness was really Anxiety, that my constant sadness was really Depression, that a few bad habits were actually Obsessive-Compulsive Disorder, and that my stomach trials were eternally linked to all of those things and more. The earliest entries here come from my days in elementary school, when I first started to show significant signs of fear, and they continue until I grew older and continued to progress along a path of Anxiety. It wasn't until years later that I began to understand how damaging and dangerous these conditions and symptoms were in my own life and the lives of others around me. These journal entries, however, became such a valuable resource in beginning to address those realities. In some passages, such as the very first entry that shows she felt anxious before I was even born, words related to anxiety actually appear. In others, I can deeply feel the very presence of anxiety, even if the word is not said.

March 6, 1984

Dear Baby,
Your arrival is anxiously awaited by everyone, your parents, grandparents and all other family and friends.

September 6, 1990

Dear Matthew,
This morning we had such a sweet but sad experience. You love school and want to go play, learn and have fun but it's still hard to let go of me. You're a little nervous but trying hard to hide it. You only ate half your (Teenage Mutant Ninja) Turtles cereal which I know you love. You gagged and almost threw up, but insisted you were fine. When I took you in to class you hugged and kissed me three or four times. There were tears in your eyes. You wanted to stay but you wanted me to stay too. It was one of those bittersweet moments that only a mother really understands. I just want you to know I love you very much.

Love,
Mom

February 1, 1991

Dear Matthew,

As I met you at the bus stop today, you got off and I could tell you were about to cry. Then you did, and I asked you what was wrong. A boy had picked on you…

June 26, 1991

Dear Matthew,

I thought you were going to quit swim lessons yesterday. You cried and was afraid to put your head under water…

May 8, 1995

Dear Matthew,

You're feeling much better physically, hardly coughing but mentally, you're still nervous and worried. I'm trying to help but it's not working. You get upset at the least little irritation lately and say you're tired of living. When I get upset you say it's not the end of the world. I guess it's just adolescence.

I love you!
Mom

January 6, 1999

Dear Matthew,

Today is your first day back to school after the holidays. I've seen increasing worry and nerves. You must break this cycle. I have been there. It's not easy. Stop now, enjoy life and let God truly be your Savior.

Love,
Mom

October 25, 2017

Dear Matthew,

From the moment I was expecting with you, I knew you were special. I knew you were going to do amazing things. I am constantly blown away by all you have accomplished. I am amazed by your abilities. I am blessed by you as a son. I love you! I believe you have many more wonderful things in your future. I expect you to be even stronger than you are now. God made you who you are and gave you many talents to still be realized. Your purpose in life will continue to touch other lives.

I love you!

You bless me.

Mom

As if my mother had not given me enough gifts by giving me life and biblical encouragement and love all these years, she also gave me the journal with so many of her thoughts and observations of my life. Reading these words that were felt in her heart and written on pages over many years really brought the trials of my mind and body to life. After reading them and pondering how I've felt for so long, I developed a realization and understanding of just what I've been dealing with and hiding from myself and from other people. The journal really did help me understand my challenges much better.

I hope this book of my own experiences will indeed, as mom said, touch other lives. I pray you will gain insight and comfort from reading about my life and realize more about your mental health and your value in this world. Though I gain great perspective on just how much I've struggled with myself and with others all my life, I also feel great hope that I have continued to live and impact other people for the better. I hope that continues with this work.

My mother's journal is evidence that I have always been a mama's boy. I deeply wanted to stay by her side when I was a boy, and the more bullies I encountered—whether on the bus, at the city swimming pool, in the school building or elsewhere—the more I wanted to stay with her. After starting a career as a public and private school teacher, she was a homemaker for much of my childhood, and there were many times when I wish I would've been homeschooled, as my wife was in her grade school years. In the end, I actually believe, however, that going to school kept me from burrowing even deeper into my shell, despite the torture I felt from the experiences I had. I am an introvert and a shy man still, even more so since I've realized just how much being in situations around people makes me anxious and nervous and paranoid about embarrassment. But if I hadn't gone to school all those years, I would've had even more of a desire to keep to myself. It would've been very difficult as an adult to go out into the world on my own, which I did successfully accomplish immediately after college.

I'm proud to be a mama's boy, something that will always be a part of me, as will my mother's cooking. Earlier I called my mom a machine in the art of ministering to me through devotions and biblical readings. She's just as much of a machine in the kitchen and in all her housework. I believe all her years as a professional homemaker—and I don't say professional with any type of jest—bred her into an expert in all kinds of skills. Mom has been a teacher, an artist and a nonprofit businesswoman in her lifetime, but I can speak from my own experiences that she is a world-class housewife and cook! Her skills in the kitchen continue to amaze me.

As far back as I can remember, my mom would have a meal ready for my dad when he came home from work every day. If she was home during the day, it was something fresh. If she was going to be away from the house for much or all of the day, she had leftovers prepared for him to quickly and easily heat when he came through the door. Sometimes, it was a combination that she called "newovers," a mixture of leftovers and new additions that together made a complete meal. I grew up on mom's cooking because we only went out to eat about two times a week—once on Saturdays after working at the homestead and once on Sundays after morning church service. Everything else was a meal at home or a meal made at home and taken to work or school. Sometimes I'd buy my lunch at school, but especially in the early years I'd take my lunchbox with something mom made me.

In more recent years, I think all that cooking has taxed mom as she's often said she feels less creative and inspired in the kitchen. But I think I appreciate her cooking now more than ever, both through recipes I make that she created or passed on to me, or through the creativity in the kitchen that I've developed by constantly cooking on my own and then for my wife. We only dine out about once or twice a week now, so we mostly consume meals made at home. The kitchen has become the place where I've come to glean a lot of therapy. I've always enjoyed cooking and eating, but as I've come to better understand my mental health challenges, I've really started to feel the therapeutic value of creating food. That's become especially true since I've become more of a homemaking husband with a few creative occupations on the side that better cater to my mental health needs. Those changes have actually led me to lovingly refer to myself as Junious Cleaver, a parody of 1950s TV housewife June Cleaver of "Leave it to Beaver."

The "house husband" reference is something I felt ashamed of for a long time, but I've come to embrace it as much as I can, and I have Mom to thank for that. She might be a machine, but she's not a robot. Manmade robots, at least in this day and age, can't feel and reciprocate emotions like my mother can. Mama was the first person who taught me to love and to appreciate and to care and to cherish other people. She taught me to hug softly because women don't like to be squeezed to death. She taught me to prize advice God gives us throughout the Bible. And she taught me to cook. All the basic arts and sciences of kitchen creativity that I use often came from my mother. Actually, everything about me, including my anxieties, originally came thanks to the delivery of my mother. And I will always strive to be grateful for that, even when I'm dealing with challenges that are a deep part of who I am.

Little Chrissy Cakes (Homemade Oatmeal Cream Cookies)

There's nothing wrong with store-bought treats. My Grandma Vember ate so many snack cakes off store shelves that she should have been given complimentary stock. Our family has also consumed more than our fair share of purchased oatmeal cream cookies, and they're quite delicious. But they pale in comparison to my mother's homemade version, which she's made at Christmastime for as long as I can remember. Mom makes a lot of homemade "goodies" for the holidays, but these are probably my favorite. They're a treat I'd miss if I didn't have them around Christmas, so I had to learn to make them myself. They take just a little more time than simply unwrapping a package, but they're so worth it.

What you need:

For the cookies
- 3 ½ cups oats
- 2 eggs
- 1 ¼ cup un-sifted all-purpose flour
- 1 teaspoon baking soda
- 1 cup soft butter or margarine
- ¼ cup sugar
- ¾ cup dark brown sugar
- 1 package instant vanilla pudding mix

For the filling
- 1 pound confectioner's sugar
- ½ cup softened butter
- 1 ½ teaspoon vanilla

What you do:
1. For the cookies, combine the butter, sugar and pudding mix in a bowl. Beat until creamy.
2. Add eggs and mix.

3. Gradually add flour mixed with baking soda.
4. Stir in your oats.
5. Roll into a 2-inch (in diameter) log and chill. (It can be frozen for up to 1 month.)
6. When you're ready to bake the cookies, slice the log into quarter-inch pieces and place them on a lightly greased cookie sheet.
7. Bake at 350 degrees for about 10 minutes until lightly browned. We like ours a little chewy, so we don't overbake them.
8. Cool on a wire rack.
9. For the filling, cream the butter and add the sugar slowly. Then beat the mixture until smooth and creamy.
10. Add the vanilla and mix well.
11. Spread a good amount between two cookies.
12. Wrap the sandwiched cookies individually. We usually use plastic wrap.
13. The cookies can be kept at room temperature and last a while, but they're freshest within the week you make them.

Moist Icebox Birthday Cake

Birthday cakes are like the people they celebrate—they come in all kinds of shapes and sizes. They also have a variety of flavors. What I consider to be my personal favorite annual cake to celebrate my birthday is much different than most. It doesn't really have icing, it doesn't need to be served with ice cream, and I believe most people nowadays have never tasted anything like it. My mother made me a moist, creamy, coconut-milky cake years ago for my birthday, and it has stuck as my cake each October. Every year I ponder other cake options, sometimes scouring recipes for hours to research potential options, but I always come back to this one. It's partially due to tradition now, but that tendency rests on the fact that this cake is so satisfying—and it becomes more delicious the longer it sits in the refrigerator. You can take great liberties, too, with this cake. You can add coconut shavings on top, or you can leave them off. You can even switch from a base vanilla cake to a chocolate version—and it's just as good with a totally different flavor. This cake seems like something the ladies at a church function would bake and eat together decades ago on a hot summer day in the South. It's sweet, cool and light enough that a sizable piece doesn't leave you feeling stuffed. It's become the only cake I imagine as my birthday treat, and I have Mom to thank for that delightful piece of my life.

What you need:
- 1 box white cake mix
- 1 can sweetened condensed milk
- 1 small can (about 8 ounces) Pina Colada mix, also called cream of coconut but not coconut milk

What you do:
1. Prepare cake as box directs.
2. Mix sweetened condensed milk with Pina Colada mix.
3. When cake is baked, remove from oven and poke holes all over the cake. (Mom uses a wooden spoon handle.)
4. Pour sweet milk and Pina Colada mix all over the cake.

5. Cool thoroughly.
6. Cover with Cool Whip.
7. Optional: Sprinkle with thawed frozen coconut.
8. Store chilled. Best when made a day ahead.

FROM HOPELESS TO HEALING

My mother gets a very significant portion of the credit for giving me life and encouraging me to be the best version of myself that I can be. Most of the remaining credit goes to my wonderful wife Molly, whom I first met when I was twenty-seven years old and already had eighty percent of my journalism career behind me. I mention the newspaper years of my life again here because that's where Molly and I met. She started as a news clerk and then progressed to being a reporter while I was the city editor at a daily paper in western North Carolina. I've been poked and prodded with the notion that we dated while I was her middle manager, but that just wasn't the case. We started dating after I had already left that employer. She soon left it, too, and moved on with her professional and personal life. But we never moved on from each other, and my life has continued and vastly improved thanks to her care and determination.

I firmly believe that if every man in this vast world could have God's guidance and the love of two women—his mother and his wife—then he would have the best shot at having a successful life that a male can have. I am incredibly lucky and blessed to say that I have always had the tremendous motherly influence of Mom in my life the whole way and several years ago added a second incredible influence into my life when I met and married Molly. The two of them get along so well, for which I'm fortunate and grateful as it's not always the case with wives and mothers-in-law—or anyone with in-laws—and both of them bring different generation-spanning female experiences to my perspective that make me a better man and a better person. If all mothers and children in-law got along as well from the start as Mama and Molly, our families and world would be so much stronger.

Where my mother always kept reminding me, and still does, that I am a talented and blessed and capable and strong man, my wife has agreed with those perspectives and added to them. She has become a guiding force that I should keep going in life, not just along whatever the world tells me I should do but on the path of what God plants in my heart to do. My wife is always guided by God, just as my mother is, and that's such a powerful thing to witness. Single young men that are looking for a woman in your life, you're doing it wrong if you're looking for sex appeal, sophistication, money or power. There are plenty of women out there who have those traits and those offerings and absolutely no substance and no strength. A strong woman is the one who understands who she is, embraces it and doesn't try to be like the rest. She doesn't care about doing all the things the world tells her she should be doing to be successful, flashy and impressive. God is her guide, and she's happy when she follows His lead. A great woman is faithful and loving and compassionate. If you don't have those things in a woman, then you need to politely decline further advancement with your current female engagement and keep looking. I'm incredibly blessed that my wife and my mother both fit that description. I believe God kept me single, unmarried that is, until I found the qualities in a wife that I always prized so much in my mother. I'm lucky to come from a family line that includes a lot of strong marriages. My dad's parents and my mom's parents were both married for decades, only separated by death. My parents and my wife's parents are both working on forty-year marriages. Now, my wife and I have goals to happily reach the same milestones someday. A strong woman and a strong marriage do great things for a man, and I desperately needed those things in my life.

Before I met Molly and dated and married her, I did not take care of myself well at all. Physically, I ate way too much, neglected exercise nearly all the time, spent too much time worrying and working, straining my body and pushing myself to always keep working harder at all costs. Other than knowing I was a child of God and a son of my parents, I didn't have a guiding force to propel me into the future in a healthy way. I knew I wanted to go to Heaven when I die, and I knew I wanted to see my parents grow old, but what else did I have to look forward to? I know that sounds like a crazy question. What else? You're striving for Heaven and seeing your parents live long lives and you want something more? Yeah, I realistically think I needed one more piece to complete the essential puzzle of me. There's a reason why we call a spouse our other half. I firmly believe, after a few years of marriage experience now, that the right spouse completes you as a person. That's why they say a husband or wife complements you, but they don't duplicate you. My wife held the missing pieces of me that encouraged me to take care of myself, to be good to my mind and body. I know this because before her, I didn't really make an effort to be caring mentally or physically to myself. I just surged forward, working as many hours as I needed and filling in the gaps with whatever food and other activities I could stand. In the news business, once I became an editor, it was normal for me to work eighty-hour weeks with few breaks and to skip most meals before devouring large dinners. And all of that came for meager salaried paychecks with no option for overtime. To put it simply, the environment and conditions were very bad for someone with anxiety, and I was guilty of just holding myself and my health to the fire for years.

A couple years after Molly and I married, I started to experience some significant strains at my job. There were a lot of changes in my career, and a new perspective and a lot of new people in my workplace. Most days, I felt my efforts were belittled, degraded and downplayed from most angles. As much as I tried to use my creative talents, they never seemed to be enough or the right fit for the place and time and people. It always seemed like somebody wanted more and something different than what I was doing. For the first time in my life, I felt like I was working incredibly hard mentally and failing at every turn. People in the office were talking about each other's shortcomings and complaining in circles about each other. The whole environment became divisive, and that really attacked my mental health at a critical and dangerous level. I had worked in newspapers before and experienced incredible adversity, but I had never been in a place where the advertised values and goals didn't match the efforts, attitude and workplace atmosphere. Everything felt completely out of whack, and that made me frantic about my whole life, even though everything at home was okay. My marriage was blissful, but things all day at work were maddening. I left stressed out of my mind every day, fearful to return because I knew it would be a challenge just to navigate a growing list of meetings, what felt like an impossible list of assignments, questions about everything under the sun in the organization and a group of people who were just not getting along the way a different set of people used to in the same place. Things felt skewed, and the constant questions about goals and the measure of success for those goals left me feeling like a complete failure. I lost all interest in creativity in my life. I didn't feel capable of anything anymore, not just at my job, but also at writing, artistic endeavors, cooking and every other hobby in my life. My creativity had died, and I felt like I was dying with it.

Around this same time, Molly and I went through several challenges in regard to acquaintances in our personal lives. The encounters with these people left us both exhausted and damaged mentally, spiritually and emotionally on an individual level. We held tight together during those challenges, and our love and support for each other never, not even for a day, waned. But the combination of those battles and the workplace stress really took its toll on me and Molly. I started to crumble under the weight, added with several other personal and professional responsibilities at the time, and I felt myself beginning to break. There came days when I felt like I couldn't get out of bed or leave the house or interact with people—and many days I didn't at a point. At times I felt like I didn't even want to live anymore—it felt like I had been devalued and put down so much personally and professionally that I couldn't produce or provide anything to the world that mattered anymore. And creativity was always the hallmark of my existence that made me feel so alive. How could I have no creativity left? I felt like a pen that had run out of ink and was outdated because no refills were being made.

My preference became being home with very little human interaction, either in person or on the phone. I drew within myself and didn't want anyone to break my forcefield. Every time any piece of adversity arose, I felt my blood start to boil. If I had to venture out in public, I was nervous I would see someone and they would ask me how I was doing and what I was doing with my life. At that time, I had taken a hiatus from a conventional career, and the few people I explained that to clearly didn't understand. So how could I even begin to explain it over and over? Why does everybody want to know about your current career more than anything else? We never ask someone about their mental health first. We don't ask about physical health either unless something has happened in the past to make it relevant. No, we always probe about a person's current job and career trajectory, as if that's all that matters. Well, that and kids and where you have a mortgage seem to be the key topics. The only other thing of interest seems to be the weather, and that feels like the measuring stick of how insignificant small talk becomes.

When someone would prod me about my career or latest accomplishments, I'd start to panic. At a point, I stopped wanting to see any people because I feared even encountering such a conversation. I was paranoid about seeing people I knew because I didn't want to be approached or seen and acknowledged. I got just as nervous and upset when things in the house or on the car would break. I'd freak out if someone would do something rude to make life difficult for me or my wife or my parents. So many things upset me and caused my anxiety and depression to spiral downward into panic. I always felt squeezed, as if I were in the grip of a workbench vice. Time seemed to fly by, and I never seemed to do anything fast enough. So many years of daily, weekly, monthly and yearly school and workplace deadlines had almost made me crazy, and I felt like I was always on the clock for everything I went to do in life, even things as simple as completing the laundry. Like the scene in "Star Wars: A New Hope" where Han Solo, Luke Skywalker and Chewbacca are trapped in the Death Star ship's garbage compactor and the walls begin closing in on them, the walls of time and the world felt like they were always closing in on me. Everything made me frantic because I felt like a failure for feeling such anxiety and depression, and for feeling a sense of failure and guilt for failed parts of my career, relationships in my past, and all the opportunities in which I'd come up short or left on the table altogether. I felt fear over my past and over my future, and I felt helpless and hopeless for any improvement, despite knowing that I had the love of God, my wife and my parents to support me. How did I become so damaged while being so blessed? I was so incredibly lost.

All this time, my wife Molly stayed by my side. She dealt with me hitting myself in frustration, constantly sitting in the restroom with a nervous stomach, worrying about everything I could possibly worry about and more. She loved me, she hugged me and kissed me, and she told me things would be all right. She prayed for me and reminded me how much God loves me, just like Mama used to do in her own ways. And at a point, my wife suggested it was time to take some time to take care of myself, to get myself in better health, both mentally and physically. She was telling me things I had always needed to hear, and she was telling them to me often. I now see and understand that God gave me the exact mother I needed, and he followed that up by giving me the exact wife I needed. For many years, I thought I would never find a wife, but God just needed to guide me to the right woman at just the right time. For all the positive and growth-guiding experiences of relationships in the past, none of the girls I dated before I dated the woman who would become my wife could even compare. Other women in the world didn't have the substance and the understanding I needed. I truly believe only Molly could have become my wife and stayed my wife, even based on just the few years we've already been married. She has the determination to see me succeed at being happy and healthy, and that stubborn determination is exactly what I needed when I had lost it myself. At a point, I entirely lost the will to live, even at a minimal level. But Molly never gave up on me.

My wife also brought a new dimension to my life that fit well with who I already was and filled in a gap that had always perplexed and eluded me. That dimension was baking, something I had always intentionally avoided in every way possible. I have long been comfortable cooking so many different things, but I have forever sidestepped any kind of baking at all costs! Not only has it eluded me, but it has absolutely frightened me. It's like I've always been all right working on the stovetop and in the microwave and with most any other kitchen appliance that would heat or reheat food, but not the oven itself. And that fear of the oven was especially true in reference to making desserts, any kind of baked goods. I loved eating them, but don't dare ask me to make them.

In contrast to my fear of baking, Molly has been cooking desserts, particularly baking pies, since she was barely a teenager. She's picked up quite a few pie recipes already in her early years, and it became her specialty, one of her favorite foods to make and consume. Ten times out of ten she'd choose a pie over a cake if given the ability to make a selection. I can comfortably say I'd make the same choice nine times out of ten. As much as we loved our incredibly delicious and beautiful wedding cake, I now wonder how we didn't somehow find a way to have pie at our reception. There are a few cakes my mom makes that would crack a list of my all-time favorite desserts and keep it from being a perfect pie sweep. But I still relish a great slice of pie whenever given the opportunity. There's just something about pastry and filling that warms my heart, my stomach and my mind in a comforting way.

While I was spending a lot of time to myself and on hiatus from any kind of real career, at least any kind that other people deem meaningful, I felt the itch to make a pie. I knew Molly was the baker in our house, and she had talked about the dream of someday owning a pie shop, but I just had the urge to make a pie one day myself. So, I looked through a stack of our recipes in cookbooks and on recipe cards, and I found Molly's basic Chess Pie recipe. As if that wasn't enough of a challenge for a guy who's always feared baking and battled intense anxiety in all corners of his life, I felt a deep desire to make my own crust, too. I knew nothing about that process, other than what I'd seen and heard my mother talk about in her kitchen, but I decided it was important that I be able to make my own crust to truly make a pie that was homemade.

So, I got my ingredients together and pulled out a clear glass deep-dish pie plate and set out to making a crust and the Chess Pie filling. Flour went everywhere. I rolled out a crust mixture, and it was a complete mess. I mashed it all back together and tried again, and it was still a mess, not even close to resembling a pie of any kind, let alone something that would look picture-worthy enough to share with anyone else. I tried a third time, and the crust rolled out fairly flat, and I succeeded in shaping it into the bottom of the pie pan. Then, I filled it with the Chess recipe, and I baked it. We tried some, and it was very tasty. Perhaps it seems like making that pie was just a baking exercise to most people, but for me, that was the first moment in which I felt healing in my mental illness journey. At the time I had felt so destroyed mentally and so discouraged about continuing in life, no matter how many encouraging people closely surrounded me. When I finally turned that mound of flour and other ingredients into pie dough and turned that dough into a crust that yielded a fabulous pie, I started to feel a little bit of life in me. And that wouldn't have happened without my wife's encouragement. She introduced me to a love of pie and an interest in making our own. In a sense, she picked up the mantle my mother had carried for years, giving me substance with which to create and a belief that I could make something meaningful and beautiful, in addition to delicious. I will always feel a kinship between me, my wife and my mother because of that daytime pie-making experience, the first one of its kind in my life. I did the actual practice of baking alone that day, but I was far from alone in my life at that point. My cooking began to heal me in the presence of my closest family members, past and present.

Encouragement to step into the kitchen and bake isn't the only push I've received from my wife during this time of intentional and hopeful healing in my life. She's also the foremost reason I went to the doctor to talk about my anxiety and depression with a medical professional. I had reached a point when solitude and reflection and meditation and the absence of stressors alone could not provide the change I needed in my life to fight my mental health battle. It had become evident that I needed a form of medical help. I had previously seen a counselor, one recommended by the same stressful employer whose counseling center had declined to advise me itself, and that person had made me feel inadequate for having any worries in my life. After one session, I closed the book on that counseling experience and didn't return for another visit. For months, I thought about other possible resources and looked shallowly into options, but I never felt comfortable with anything. Finally, I guess I felt enough panic and saw enough pain in my wife, who ached for my mind and my whole life to get better, that I felt the urge to call my family primary care doctor, tell them I had anxiety and depression concerns, and visit for a consultation and a possible prescription medication to help me deal with my mental challenges.

I dreaded that first visit so much, just like I've always dreaded every single visit I've ever made to medical offices of any kind. I'm a private person, and I've experienced so many problems with my mind, my stomach and the rest of my body that I don't want anyone touching it or probing it or prodding it or asking questions about it. The very thought creates a rising sense of panic deep within me. But

I knew by this time that I had to make some kind of change and effort to take care of myself, not just for myself but for the sake of my wife, too. I could feel her concern for me, her frustration with my lack of effort to care for myself, and her rising worry that my health might continue to atrophy past a point of help. So, I kept my appointment, talked to the doctor and received a prescription for a daily little white pill for my anxiety and depression. Just like that, I had taken a major step in trying to help myself. It was just as difficult as I always imagine every step of life will be, and I wasn't comfortable stepping into the doctor's office, but my doctor was reasonable, caring, listened to me, offered suggestions and then prescribed a medicine to try to help me. Bottom line, the doctor really listened in a nonjudgmental way and then took a step on my behalf to improve my life. Feeling that care from the doctor really made a difference for me, but feeling the care of my wife was really the biggest factor in helping my health.

In the time since that doctor visit, I've continued to take the prescription to help my brain deal with anxiety, I've increased my daily exercise, another key step in the fight against my mental illness, I've returned to creating with words by writing on topics I advocate for and enjoy, and I've improved my diet. Proudly, I can say that I have lost nearly eighty pounds and kept it off for months. I know that sounds like a major fitness fad diet ploy, but it's true. There's been no magical key to changing my health. More exercise, a better diet, eliminating as much stress as possible, taking my medicine, reading my Bible and consulting my loving family members have been the keys to turning around my health. When I have a period of deep struggle now, I retreat from all damaging dangers and draw nearer to all those things that comfort, love and protect me. I cling to my faith, my family and good food. I still have a long, long way to go, but I am so glad that I started this part of my journey.

I traveled a long way in life before God led me to my wife, but when I found her, I made the most of our meeting and our joining of hands. Molly, as I often tell her, is evidence to me that a wonderful wife, or husband if you're a woman, can be like the extension of God's love on earth in human form. When we connect with the spouse we know and feel He designed for us, we can feel His presence with us every day in mind, body and spirit. That's what my wife has done for me. She's amplified the love of God that I already felt and helped it more greatly extend to all parts of my life, most newly and notably to taking care of myself, something that was such a foreign concept in my twenties when I would work all the time without regard for my needs, eat whatever I felt like or everything that was in sight, and very rarely make any efforts to exercise. In addition to all of that, my wife has also led me to baking as a deep therapy for my mental health improvement. I can't imagine not baking now, to the point that it's actually become more of a favorite and essential part of my cooking than anything else I do in the kitchen. Every time I bake something, I think about my grandmothers and my own mother who have made so many favorite family recipes in the kitchen with the love of their hearts and hands. But after making that first pie and feeling its healing help, I believe I have my wife to thank most of all for truly broadening my horizons and for introducing me to a new way to create and give positive life to myself.

Banny's Famous Chocolate Pie

Growing up, I ate a wide variety of Southern desserts because I was raised in a family of people who knew how to work the kitchen to cook up delicious meals—and everyone also relished each opportunity to gather around the dinner table and eat. Boy, could we eat. While there were so many things we ate, I don't remember us frequently consuming a lot of pie, other than at Thanksgiving, when we enjoyed the traditional pumpkin, sweet potato, pecan and other common varieties in the South. As much as I associate almost every food with someone close to me in my family, I'm not sure I linked pie to anyone—until I met and married the woman who is now my wife. She's made pies for much of her life. She's loved pies even longer. And this chocolate pie is a very special recipe made by her great-grandmother, a woman they called Banny. It offers a filling of rich, chocolatey pudding topped with a light and airy meringue. It's a recipe that takes time to make, the kind of thing that people used to cook when they devoted more time to the kitchen and to taking care of each other. I never met Banny, like I never met many members of mine and Molly's family that came generations before us. But I feel a kinship with her when I make this pie, and that demonstrates the power of cooking and family and the stories behind recipes and traditions. Our kitchen traditions bridge the gaps of time, living on in the processes repeated through the years by different family members, continuing who we were and leading to who we become. That's what this pie represents to me.

What you need:

For the filling:
- 2 ½ tablespoons all-purpose flour
- 2 egg yolks
- 3 tablespoons cocoa
- 2 cups milk
- 1 cup sugar

- 1 teaspoon vanilla
- 1 pie crust

For the meringue topping:
- 2 egg whites
- ½ cup sugar
- 1 teaspoon vanilla

What you do:
1. Pre-cook pie crust at 350 degrees for about 10 minutes or until golden.
2. Separate the egg yolks from the egg whites, putting the whites into a small bowl and the yolks into a nonstick pot, or a double boiler, as Banny's recipe originally prescribed.
3. Add the remaining pie ingredients to the pot. Cook on medium heat until pudding consists. (Those are the original words, which mean you want the mixture to begin to thicken.)
4. Stir frequently.
5. Pour the chocolate pudding into the cooked pie crust.
6. Prepare the topping by beating the egg whites until stiff, then adding the sugar and vanilla.
7. Pour the meringue topping over the pudding layer and spread evenly.
8. Cook on 350 for about 10 minutes or until meringue is golden brown.
9. Allow to cool then refrigerate to help solidify. Keep refrigerated.
10. Best served either cold or slightly warmed.

Molly's Homemade Flour Tortillas

I still remember the first time I ate Molly's homemade tortillas during a church game night. At that time, I had never seen anyone make homemade tortillas before, other than in restaurants. My reflection on that first experience shows the powerful personal history component of food. A simple dish has the ability to transport us across space and time to another place and moment in our lives. There's something incredibly comforting about these tortillas—and they're almost more like pita bread, hearty and sturdy but warm and soft at the same time. They make a great soft taco shell for breakfast, lunch or dinner, but they can really house just about anything you like, both food and memories.

What you need:
- 2 cups tortilla flour (You can find it on the baking aisle at many grocery stores.)
- About 2/3 cup warm water

What you do:
1. Put the tortilla flour in a large bowl. Slowly add the water, mixing in with your hands until fully incorporated. Form into a large ball until all of the flour is absorbed. Cover the bowl with a damp kitchen towel, and let the dough rise for about 5 minutes.
2. Tear off and form small balls, slightly bigger than the size of a golf ball, and place them on a floured surface. You should end up with about 9 dough balls. Take each ball and roll it out with a rolling pin to about an eighth of an inch thick.
3. Heat a cast iron skillet (or a frying pan) to medium, and cook each tortilla until lightly toasted on both sides. Watch them carefully. You may want to use a fork or other utensil to flip them because they will be hot. And you may need to flip each tortilla multiple times to get them just right. Practice makes perfect.
4. You can stack them on a plate or place them in a tortilla

warmer until ready to use. It's as simple as that!

A CONNECTION TO CALM AND COMFORT

It saddens me greatly to know that many people have lifelong questions about who their parents are or where their parents are. Of all the things in my life that have caused me mental anguish, the status of my ancestry is not one of those. I've always said I have no doubt that my father and mother, as presented, are indeed my father and mother. I carry so many of their traits, both good and bad, as all children tend to do. The same can be said for my grandparents who came before them. I see so much of my parents' parents in myself, even my dad's parents who I didn't have much of a chance to know on this earth.

One exception to the traits my family has passed along to me is my Grandpa Lee's patience. The man had plenty of stress and opposition to deal with in his life, but most of the time you just couldn't tell that was the case. He was born to a poor mill family in western North Carolina. I recall him telling me stories about his childhood in the 1930s when he played with bricks in the dirt by and under the house and pretended they were cars on roadways. When he graduated from high school, he joined the Army and served in Korea. During that time, he started a courtship with the young woman from his hometown community who would become my grandmother, my mom's mother. The two of them had so much love in their lifetime, but they never had their finances fully in order, as we found out many years later when they lived out their final months, weeks and days. There was so much to be happy for and proud of—while there was also plenty to be nervous and stressed about—but there was never an absence of calm in my Grandpa Lee.

My mother always says she didn't see fear in Grandpa's eyes until near the very end. We knew he had God in his life and Jesus as the Savior in his heart, but we did see concern in him. Maybe it was physical pain. Perhaps he was just upset to leave the side of my grandma, with whom he spent fifty-nine years of marriage. I just don't know. But I know he was a calm man who didn't raise his voice often. When he was upset, you could tell by the look in his eyes. He had this stare that, to me, said, "Stop what you're doing." I noted it any time my grandma, my mom and myself would be a bit too silly for too long. My grandma's side of the family, and all her siblings, had the gift of incredible humor, and I'm certain we could "whoop and holler and carry on" way too much when we got together. Occasionally, I could tell that Grandpa had had enough. But the man still loved to talk and laugh, just not in the extremely silly way the rest of us could. I guess that's normal for a lot of men. My dad didn't let out many belly laughs when I was growing up, so when he did, I knew it was something he truly found incredibly funny.

Grandpa was just this gentle man with silvery to snowy white hair, a firm handshake and a kind voice. I can hear it now, and it makes me smile inside. Everything about him was just, as I said, calm. He told my mother he got his demeanor from his Grandpa Felix. I'm inclined to think all of us guys get a heavy dose of our grandfathers in us. My dad's work ethic and general mannerisms carry a lot of his Grandpa Gifton, a nose-to-the-grindstone, old-school farmer. And I've been called, by my mom and wife and others, a gentle giant. I attribute a lot of that quality, as well as my meekness toward others— which I humbly believe is one of my best assets to humanity—to my grandpa. I just wonder all the time why I got his kindness but somehow left God's human assembly line with my grandma's worrisome nature instead of my grandpa's calm spirit. Maybe I'll find out someday, or maybe I never will. It's something I think about often, the whole concept of how we end up with different pieces of the people who came before us and led to our lives. Likely, that very interest is why I have so much wonder for genealogy and history in general. I'm fascinated to learn about my ancestors because I, in turn, learn so much about myself. That's why my family is so inextricably linked to my faith, to food in my life and to the fears I've held so tightly.

What I lack in my grandfather's peace, I make up for in his downright love and appreciation for excellent food. The man absolutely enjoyed a good meal at every turn. Some of my favorite memories of him include a dinner table in one of our family's houses or a booth at a locally-owned restaurant. No matter what a day together entailed, there was always good food to be had, and I think that's a major reason why the experience and importance of eating are such a deep-seated part of who I am as a person.

My grandfather is responsible for introducing me to some of the most iconic restaurants in his native and lifetime home of Rutherford County in western North Carolina. The Fountain at Smith's Drugs, what he and many others historically knew as Smith's Cut Rate, and Davis Donut House, are two of my favorites to this day. I recollect sitting in a booth at Smith's, full as a tick as we like to say here in the South, still eating a fried apple pie with French vanilla ice cream. Sometimes I feel bad about the memory, actually, because it was a day when I was having a very upset stomach and had said I didn't want pie and ice cream. Can you imagine such a thing, me declining pie? What a crazy notion! But it's one of those mental images that always comes to mind when I think of fried pies or that place in time. My stomach was an enemy so many times in my youth and continues to be into my adult life. I regret its impact on me, so strong that I would tell my grandpa I didn't want dessert. He ordered me a plate anyway, and I remember eating it. I suppose I should carry forward the memory of just being there with my grandpa. As I said before, so many children don't grow up knowing their grandparents or spending quality time with them that has a positive impact on their lives, so I should be very thankful for the opportunity.

Grandpa worked in a restaurant himself as a young man, putting in time at the legendary local Windy's diner, operated by "Windy" Powell, no association with the now-famous national fast food chain with a similar name separated by only one differing letter. The place was renowned in those parts for something called a beef dog, a cuisine I remember my great-grandma, Hassie, talking about in my very young years. Basically, the sandwich was seasoned, stewed beef pulled onto a hamburger bun. We've resurrected the beef dog in recent years in our family, including its serving a few years back at a summertime cookout at my great uncle Buck's home, and it's now a must-have tradition every once in a while for me. The food makes me think of Windy, whom I never met, but even more it makes me think of my grandfather.

All these memories of food, family and local history often make me hungry, but they also do contribute a certain calm to my life through their peace from my past. Among the many nervous and upset times I've had in my life from anxiety and depression, there's so much good to remember. The connection to Grandpa was strong during his life. I always felt particularly close to him and enjoyed his presence. That has continued even after he passed away. I visit his resting place as often as I can, and always close to his birthday each April. When I'm there I usually pull up a seat and settle in to talk to him, updating him on my life, concerns I have, as well as things I can celebrate. I was most excited of all to tell him several years ago when I had married my wife Molly. He would have loved her so much. I know he still does, just from a distance in Heaven. I very much believe, because I believe firmly in the Bible, that we'll be reunited someday with our loved ones.

I'm already united in spirit with my grandpa though. I talk to him often, even when I'm not at his gravesite. When I enjoy a particularly good meal, or something that he would have absolutely loved eating, I tell him about it, wherever I am. Food has helped me maintain a connection to my grandpa, and thus a link to my past and to my roots. And that bond with my grandpa and my foundation has helped bestow on me a level of peace and comfort through all the fear and dread in my mind, even when the mental opposition has been at its worst. I think we all have so much to gain and to appreciate in where we come from. For me, a big part of who I am may be the mental challenges I've inherited from pieces of my past. But I also have my past to thank for the immense love of food that helps me enjoy life, even during times when my mind and my stomach make it more difficult to do so. I may not have my grandpa's peace, as hard as I try and as much as I want to grasp it, but I have a lot of him in me, and I take joy and pride in that.

Grandpa's Corn Casserole

Grandpa Lee was no slouch in the kitchen! He could jump right behind the stove and make some delicious dishes, including a corn casserole he made at Thanksgiving. There's just something hearty and flavorful about the casserole, and of course now it preserves special memories of him making it, which fondly rush back every time I eat it. You know how it's not a proper holiday without a certain food? As much as turkey, stuffing and pumpkin or sweet potato pie matter, it's not a perfect Thanksgiving for me without his corn casserole. My grandpa introduced it to me, as he introduced so many things that I continue to enjoy and appreciate more as the years go by. As an important note for this recipe, you can substitute fresh corn for the canned corn for an extra-special, fresh flavor.

What you need:
- 1 can cream corn
- 1 can whole kernel corn
- 2 eggs
- ½ cup cream
- ½ stick melted butter
- ½ cup cornmeal
- 1 cup shredded cheddar cheese

What you do:
1. Mix all of your ingredients, and pour the combination into a greased casserole dish.
2. Bake at 350 degrees for about 30 minutes, or until browned on top.

Windy Powell's Beef Dogs

As a young man, Grandpa Lee worked at a local restaurant named Windy's, not to be confused with the national chain. This was a special community diner right off the mill hill, owned by the iconic Windy Powell, a prominent businessman and local government leader. Mr. Powell served many delicious things in his establishment, but the most renowned and surviving memory for our family was the beef dog, a sandwich of seasoned stewed beef on a hamburger bun. I remember my great-grandma, Hassie Quinn, talking about them when I was a small boy, and I also recall my grandpa talking about them at Windy's restaurant. This recipe is entirely from Windy himself, who by modern accounts was known to prescribe every ingredient "to taste." I love that approach because it's how I most enjoy cooking in my own kitchen. Everyone has a different taste, so a recipe should let the maker decide how much of any ingredient to include. It's kind of a metaphor for life. We must decide what provides the best balance for our own lives.

What you need:
- Stew Beef
- Chili Powder to taste
- Black Pepper to taste
- Worcestershire to taste
- Hot sauce to taste
- Garlic Powder to taste
- Oregano Leaves to taste
- Chopped Onions to taste

What you do:
1. Cook beef seasoned with other ingredients until well done. In recent years, I've used a slow cooker to cook my beef when I tried out Windy's recipe.
2. Mash the beef with a potato masher into a thick mush.
3. Serve with chopped onions in a hamburger bun.

MATTHEW TESSNEAR

I AM STILL HERE, AND I WILL BE ALL RIGHT.

My father's homestead has been in our family for at least one-hundred and twenty-five years. That's something I wouldn't have appreciated many years ago, when Dad dragged me in the wee hours of weekend mornings to the property for manual labor. Now, it's a reality that I take great pride in, but also one that I feel a tremendous responsibility for into the future. That plot has survived through two world wars, the Great Depression and the Great Recession, among other challenges. It's been sustained by people with a certain gritty toughness. For me, the land symbolizes hard work, determination and history. More than a century is a long time, and I will do all I can to ensure the place remains a part of our line past my lifetime. The respect I have for my parents absolutely has a lot to do with those plans, but there's also a tremendous connection I feel for those I never met who lived on the homestead. Most notably of all those relatives is my grandmother, Lois.

She was one of three surviving daughters who inherited a third of the total family land, and her portion was the place where she and my grandpa built their house and raised my father. I feel a piercing sword in my heart when I think of her because she passed away suddenly at the age of fifty-four, three years before I was born into this world. As a child, I didn't think too much about her. What kid thinks about people he hasn't met? Maybe there's a certain interest in the world—

a familiar series of why questions. But that's about where it stops for a young man. When that little boy grows up and becomes an adult, however, he starts to desire knowing where he comes from. And that very feeling has formed an inseparable link between me and my grandmother, who never held me and whom I've never gazed upon in real life.

This is the point in my story at which I feel I am most sharing who I really am. Pieces of me go in many directions, but I feel this sense that they all gather with the topic, the very essence of my grandmother, Lois. I descend into sadness when I think about how I never got to be with my grandma, how my father was parted from his mother before he was thirty years old. As I've aged, the reality that we don't know how long we have to live has nagged and tugged and yanked at my anxiety cord. When will we all cease to exist in this world? Nobody knows! How terribly frightening that feeling can persist every single day. It's the kind of thing that makes me feel mental anguish most purely. The seed of that one little question—when will we all die?—is enough to create a million trees full of questions about everything that is and everything that could be in the entire world. And at so many points in my life that's exactly where I've been living—in a never-ending forest of fear, not being able, as they say, to see the forest for the trees. Each one, each little sapling of fear, pops up right in front of me, and I cannot get it off my mind.

People who have written about the terrible realities of anxiety have described the process as a spiral. We get one worry on our mind and can't rid ourselves of it, and then we take that road to a thousand other worrisome stops. But the pain and the piercing fear never end, and we just unravel, lost in doubts and what-ifs about our lives and the world around us. When I think about how my grandmother was taken from us, I want to cry out how much this world isn't fair. I want to know what my fate will be, down to every detail, and I won't be happy until I do. Thinking about my grandmother Lois has brought me to the place inside where these feelings live. But, in a twist of irony, I also feel most at peace when I imagine my grandmother and the life she lived on this earth, a period of time in which I didn't fully exist, at least not in body, but in which I was already destined to be.

One of the most peaceful memories in my whole life came while taking a bath in my parents' house several years back, early in my twenties. I was visiting them on a few days off from work where I lived in the eastern part of North Carolina at the time. That night while in the bathroom, the very room that was my torture chamber as a young man who strained himself in the hopes of staying far away from the bathrooms at school, I was lying quietly in the tub, and I felt my Grandma Lois's voice with me.

This isn't a ghost story. It's not about some wild supernatural experience I've had. There wasn't an audible sound of my grandmother speaking. I didn't see anything different in the room as if I were experiencing some kind of vision. Grandma's voice was more of a feeling, a spiritual movement inside of me. If someone's speaking can be in your heart and soul, this was an example of one of those times. Simply, Grandma's voice said, "It's all going to be okay. You're going to be okay."

At the time, I was in a particularly stressful period at the office. I had been working a lot of hours, and I had been spending all the remaining time in my day worrying about the work that was and the work that was to come. I was a wreck. Mentally, I was always feeling myself stretching in all the different directions others made me believe I should be moving. More! I should always be striving to do more! And all the while, I was eating my anxieties about everything in the form of incredible food binges outside of the office. I cringe now when I think about how much I poured through my body every day. So many of the physical aches and ills I have now must surely be due to what I put my body through during that time period. But here was my grandma, a woman I've never met, coming to me in a difficult time in a place that held horror-filled memories for me, telling me that my life was going to be okay. That moment in that bathtub, I felt an incredible peace descend on me. It's the greatest sense of calm

I've ever experienced, and it's my model standard for hope and happiness.

That one little moment, something that's never duplicated itself to my knowledge in the years since, was enough to cause me to want to live a little bit more. At that time, I wanted to know more about my grandmother. Suddenly, I wanted the family land that I had never had any interest in whatsoever. Though I knew life was tough, and I had an uphill battle against my mind and body, I held out hope that someday things would be better. It's taken me years—quite possibly a full decade now from that moment—but things have finally become better for me.

By no means have I "defeated" anxiety. You don't defeat anxiety for good, let me tell you from first-hand experience. You must fight it every single day and tell it to go away in a lifetime war on every front. Every time you win a battle with anxiety, you start rallying your internal troops and external armies for another round of the mental enemy's assault. Anxiety charges back at you over and over again. There's never an end to the battle. But we all have things in our lives that are valuable that we can keep in our hearts and minds that will help us continue the fight.

On the outside, someone would look at me and tell me I'm healthy, because I look healthy. They would say I have so much value in my life because I have a family homestead I'll inherit someday. They would tell me I've seen so much already in my life as a college graduate and an award-winning journalist. But none of that really matters in the war with my mind and the war that rages deep in my gut, the two foremost battlefronts in my world.

What really does matter? Well, for starters, my relationship with Jesus Christ. He's the reason I know I don't have to worry in the end. I accepted His existence and His death and resurrection, all for the purpose of saving me from my sins, and that means He has my back no matter what for all time. That alone is the most priceless thing I could ever have.

After my faith in Jesus Christ, what's of utmost value in my life?

Well, I have a pair of loving parents who have been married for decades, and now I have the most wonderful wife in all the world, and they all care so deeply about me that they've sacrificed time, talents and money to be with me and make my life better. My gosh, I'm the richest man on earth where it matters. And that's before I even count the people who came before me, like my grandmother, who have lived and died, and I am certain, from the evidence presented to me in the form of letters and photographs and stories, have gone to Heaven because of the ways they lived their lives. I can feel their presence, just like I could sense my grandma Lois tell me that day in the bathtub that I would be okay. And you know what? She was right. I am still here, and I will be all right.

My experience with my grandmother that night, now years ago, came not long after my mother had shared with me a set of love letters exchanged between Grandma Lois and Grandpa Harry during his service to the United States Army during World War II. The letters are quite possibly, along with my family Bibles and my wedding ring, the most priceless tangible possessions I own. Soon after Mom gave the envelopes to me, I took them back to my home in Eastern North Carolina and on a day off from work carried them with me to a nearby riverfront beach, where I sat in a chair, read them to myself and cried tears of happiness. It was the first time I had met my grandmother, and I was meeting her in the past, where she lived most vividly of all.

Now, sometimes when I'm in the house my father's parents once inhabited, I find myself lingering in the kitchen. It's the place where my Grandma Lois cooked many of the meals she made as an adult. She lived in that house from about the age of twenty-four, coincidentally the same age as my wife when she and I married, until she passed away thirty years later. It's from that very kitchen that, through my parents' gifts, I received her pie plates, her recipe box and a few other of her cooking implements. Of course, when I use each of them, I think of her with warm, fond memories. And I catch myself having hope.

Grandma was a wonderful cook, my parents tell me. Now, my wife tells me I'm a wonderful cook. If Molly and I are lucky enough to have children, I imagine and dream that they'll someday remember me as a fine cook. Of all the people who contribute to my strength to overcome anxiety, to better myself, even in the midst of life's adversity and the nips and rips of people who have bad intentions in the world because for some reason they haven't felt the desperate need for giving kindness and gentleness to everyone we meet, Grandma Lois, even as I have not felt the touch of her hugs, powers me the most. Maybe it's because I know she felt pain, too. That discomfort extended throughout my family to my Grandpa Harry and my father, then my mother, then her parents, my other grandparents, touching us all. And it has now reached me, too, but through that incredible pain, I also feel her hope and her love. She oozed sweetness and generosity and faithfulness in those letters she penned to my grandpa when they were hundreds, sometimes thousands, of miles away. She was sweeter than the finest sugar or honey, words she used to address the man who became my grandpa.

With each roll of the pin on the counter, each sprinkle of salt and pepper into dishes, each stir of cream in my coffee, I quite literally think of my Grandma Lois. I believe I have so much of her in me because I can feel her presence always. For my life, she is where everything comes together, the anxiety and the hope, even though I never met her in person. And in the acreage our family continues to own and maintain, there is a beautiful reminder that everything we do and everything we feel, the good and the bad, all has a purpose, a meaning, a value for us and all the people who come down the line. There have been times when I have imagined how much I wish I had never been born, how much I wanted to take myself out of this life, when I just couldn't take the immense pressure and failure I felt any longer, and I pleaded with God to go ahead and take me, that I was ready to exit the stage of this world. But He hasn't answered my pleas yet. He knows when it's time for me to go, just like He knew when it was time for Him to call my grandma home to be with Him. He has never-ending providence over my life the same way he did with my grandma. He gave her a number of years on this earth, and in that time, He guided her to give birth to my father, and then He helped my father make me.

Life always goes on when we allow it to, and when we let God do His job, which is overseeing everything in existence, including our own lives, some pretty amazing things can happen. I know I've seen that in my own life. When I think back to all those days in my youth and young adulthood when I battled incredible pain and anguish over what I had to face at school or work that coming day, I marvel at where God has me now. For all the anxiety and resulting depression I've endured, I have my ancestry, my parents, my wife and the family homestead to enjoy and in which to take pride. I have so many blessings, things that are more than just tangible people, places and things. And the blessings really do drown out the sound of the nagging anxieties in my mind and in my belly. Those fears can't take away the reality that I am and will always be who I am. All I have to do is remember that, and I'll be okay, just like my grandma said. And since I'm going to be who I am, I'm going to keep cooking and eating, but I'm going to do it at a healthy pace.

I think it took me until the age of thirty-three to actually realize who I really am. I am a man named Matthew who has a mental illness called anxiety. I also deal with depression, Chronic Fatigue Syndrome, Obsessive-Compulsive Disorder, Post-Traumatic Stress Disorder and Irritable Bowel Syndrome. There are so many flaws, I can't keep track of them all. But like I said, there are so many more blessings that overshadow the challenges.

For many years, I didn't allow myself to see who I was and what I needed. I tried to hide all my mental and physical imperfections, in the hope that others wouldn't notice them but also erroneously in the hope that I wouldn't have to face them. By the time I reached my thirties, I had stuffed so much truth about my life into a closet that it all came flowing out the door. There was too much to hide anymore. That's when I cleaned out the closet, gave it all away and started to restock the shelves with only the things that were most essential to living my best life, the one that Matthew was destined to live.

There comes a time in life when a person develops a desire for self-preservation, a deep longing to enjoy as much health and happiness as possible with other humans who share mutual love and support. I'm glad to say that time has come for me. So many people don't realize the importance of taking care of mind and body until traditional retirement age in the sixties and seventies, or even later. It's a gift, even along a difficult road that I've made into a treacherous path at many points in my journey, to understand the crucial nature of self-care and of taking care of the people who have loved and nurtured me.

This self-preservation process has included the difficult task of letting go of things and people who inhibit me from living my best life. Sadly, I must be honest with myself and with you that I've crossed paths with quite a few other human beings who do not have the best intentions for my life and even for their own lives. There can be quite a destructive impact from constant contact with people who infuse intentional negativity and physical or mental pain through words and actions. While it's been difficult, my efforts to clean out the closet of my own hidden health problems has also included a purging of relationships that have been particularly damaging for me. That's difficult to do and say, but there comes a time when such a thing can make the difference between life and death from a mental strain standpoint.

Sometimes we hear people talk about the meaning of life. Well, I've figured out what that is now, best I can tell. It only took me thirty-plus years of wandering around in the dark to turn on the light and discover it, even when I had all kinds of tools at my disposal. Here's what I've found, the secret I've discovered:

We get one chance to live on this earth. In that time, we can only be ourselves. No matter how hard we try our best to morph ourselves into something else to meet our desires and the wants and needs of other people, we can only successfully be the person we actually were designed by God to be. I believe God created each one of us uniquely to enjoy this life as His gift and to also better the lives of all the people He leads us to encounter. Grandpa Lee always gave people a marble to remember him by. What people really remember about us, the metaphorical marble, is how we make them feel when they're around us. We get many chances to make a positive impact on people, through our love and gentleness, in the years God gives us in our lives. Then, He calls us to be with Him. That's all there is to it, I'm convinced. What a simple existence life actually can be when that's how we see it. That realization is similar to the feeling I had when I could sense my grandma telling me everything would be okay.

I'm still breathing, and my heart's still beating. That means I'm not done living yet. So, I'm going to keep sharing a marble of kindness with those I meet, whenever I can. I'm going to keep doing the things God has placed on my heart to do, the actions like cooking that connect me to my true self and allow me to share gentleness and hope with those around me. At times in my life, anxiety has quite literally been a force that has been eating me alive. But it has not defeated me. And now, with more perspective on who I am, where I came from and what I have to live for, I can cook and eat with more peace and more hope that mental illness will not overcome me. I will overcome it, and I will live.

Grandma Lois's Sweet Baked Stickies

Like I said, I never got to meet Grandma Lois. So, like Grandma Vember, I don't have memories of her instructing me how to make her delicious recipes in the kitchen. From talking to my family members, however, I have procured a basic understanding of a few of her specialties, and I have a few of her recipes, too. One of those is for something called "Stickies," basically a biscuit dough sweetened with lots of vanilla and sugar. The key with these, as my dad says, is that you can't add too much sugar or vanilla. I don't know exactly how my Grandma Lois made her biscuits, so I usually go with my wife Molly's recipe for simple biscuits and then add the sweetener and flavor.

What you need:
- 2 cups self-rising flour
- ½ cup shortening
- ¾ cup buttermilk
- Sugar to taste
- Vanilla to taste

What you do:
1. Preheat your oven to 450 degrees.
2. Blend the flour and shortening with your hands, then stir in the milk.
3. Work the mixture until you have a dough.
4. On a floured surface, roll out the dough until you have a flat sheet, almost like you would a pie crust.
5. Sprinkle a generous heap of sugar and vanilla on the dough sheet.
6. Roll up the sheet, encasing all of the sugar and vanilla inside.
7. Slice the roll of dough into quarter-inch pieces or so.
8. Bake at 450 for about 10 minutes, or until browned as you like.
9. Serve with cold glasses of milk or warm cups of coffee.

Essie's Egg Custard Pie

Many years ago, when I was a boy, long before I started making pies myself, I remember my mom making egg custard pie because my dad loved it. I didn't really understand at the time that the pie was a recipe straight from my great-grandmother, Essie McCombs, who lived on the farm that adjoins my father's homestead that remains in our family today. My wife believes custard pies are more of an old-fashioned treat that don't suit the tastes of many eaters today, and I agree. But I can't imagine how anyone can't enjoy the simplicity of this pie. The first time I made miniature tart versions of it, I took my great-aunt Betty, my late grandmother Lois's sister, one at her home. She told me it tasted right, and I told her the recipe was her mother's. She said her mom would use ingredients from the farm in her egg custard pie when they were available. I think about that when I make this pie, and I take great pride in having my great-grandmother's recipe. She was the woman who created my grandmother, who created my father, who created me. That passing down of people leads to a passing down of history and of recipes. Thinking about where I came from gives me great peace, and I believe that's why I enjoy eating family recipes so much. They connect me with the past and who I am in the present.

What you need:
- 4 eggs
- ¾ cup sugar
- 1 ½ cup milk
- 2 tablespoons flour
- ½ teaspoon vanilla
- ¼ stick butter, cut into pieces
- 1 unbaked pie crust

What you do:
1. Dissolve the flour into the milk.
2. Add the beaten eggs, sugar and flavoring.
3. Add the butter pieces, not melted.

4. Bake at 425 degrees for 5 minutes.
5. Reduce the heat to 350 and bake 35 more minutes until set and golden brown. The pieces of butter will help provide a browning on top.

"Have faith in God," Jesus answered.

— Mark 11:22

AFTERWORD

During an earlier version of this book, I wrote a section that began with a realization that my life is pretty "F'd up." Quite literally, I meant that all of the most influential elements of my existence have been best categorized into words that begin with the letter F. In processing all of the necessary mental revisions to put together a first draft, I edited out that musing, then I remembered it and discovered it was perfect to explain here in an afterword of sorts. I say afterword because there's no conclusion to my story. Because I keep living, I keep battling anxiety. It's who I really am. Faith, family, food, fear, all those things and more make up me as a person. I cannot change that, but I have embraced it at what I hope is a more aware and healthier level.

This book has undergone several major revisions before even becoming a first draft for my editor, my gracious and incredibly well-read wife Molly, to read. While the previous versions had value, they didn't say as a whole what I needed them to say. As much as I appreciate you sharing this journey with me by reading all these pages, this work has most of all been a valuable cathartic process for helping me remember who I am, where I came from and what I will always be. As the book has changed, so has my life. This volume's varying pages is a comparison to my life, which goes through its own stages and revisions constantly. I am always the person I've always been, but I continue to grow and adapt, experience loss, accept additions and all manner of changes. That's been an important lesson for me during this creative process.

Writing has been a deep therapy for me over the months I've worked earnestly on this book. I've typed so much on the computer on which all these words have been created that I've worn the most-used letters off the keys. And every second I've put into it has helped me more completely understand just who I am as a person. That is enough value alone for me to say that this book is a success. Each reader will take his or her opinion away from these pages, but I already feel a sense of accomplishment because this project has helped me better appreciate the person I am and the life I have been gifted to live.

My mother always said I had a book in me. Well, mom, here it is. And guess what? The taste of completion has already led me to look forward to publishing subsequent stories—both real life and fictional—that are knocking on the door of my brain. I've already answered a few of the stories' request for entry, and I'm sitting down entertaining their proposals. In other words, I am always writing on something, with the hope that each moment will become part of something that finds its way out into the world for other eyes and minds and hearts. But most of all, the writing itself is the end goal because it helps me to release my thoughts, and releasing my thoughts, whether through speaking them or putting them on a digital or printed page has become a very important factor in maintaining my sanity. There are many forms of counseling in this world. Sitting down with my thoughts and an open word-processing document just might be the most effective for a writer like me. Thank you, Mom, for being the first to encourage me that writing is a talent I possess and that writing is an art and that art has value. To me, you will always be the greatest artist who has ever lived.

I must also thank my wife Molly for lovingly staying by my side during this entire process, including all the days when I struggled to exist and accept who I am. Molly met me before I hit an anxiety wall that required me to stop jogging around it and start climbing over it, but she never left me, even when I crashed at full speed into that wall. I don't know that I'll ever actually scale the barrier, but I am definitely perched higher on it now, and I'm going to keep propelling upward, even when life tries to knock me off. Molly, you'll always be my 42, the answer to life, the universe and everything.

My father and all of my grandparents also merit and receive my deepest appreciation and love for all they have poured into me. Your sacrifices, your struggles, your celebrations, everything about your lives is not in vain. You have made me who I am, and I am now proud of all of it. None of my life would be possible, quite literally, without you and the back-breaking work you have done. Thank you, from the very depths of my heart.

I would also like to thank all my teachers, both traditional educators and others who have encouraged me as a writer and seeker of knowledge. That includes you, Becky Ballard, Doris Chapman, Janie Dunsmore, Weeta Garner, Carol Lowry, Catherine Pace, John Rains, Doris Rhyne, Kitty Saunders, Nancy-Pat Scanlon, Harriet Sifford and so many others past, present and future.

I also want to thank Kim and Clyde Millman, who started Kim's Kitchen in Stanley, North Carolina so many years ago. Your hard work, love for people and dedication to service have been a gift to our family and to my life for so many years of delicious food and memories. You will have a special place in our family story for all time, and you are majorly responsible, along with my father, for my love of cheeseburgers. And, along with pie, burgers are the food that will always be a form of edible therapy for me, even on my most difficult days.

Finally, I must, surprisingly even to myself, thank the people who have made my journey difficult. You are part of an army that has wounded me but never defeated me. Among you are the boys who scattered the contents of my backpack all over the ground as a frightened kindergarten bus rider, the teenagers who held me at the bottom of the pool during swim lessons I never completed as a child, and all the adults who have condescended, belittled and lorded possessions and achievements over me in attempts to crack my own confidence. Simply put, you have hurt me, but that has also made me who I am, and in the end, it has eventually helped me realize just how strong and valuable I have really become.

If I have left anyone influential out, please accept my apologies. Everyone I have met has impacted who I am. That's the truth of our lives. We all touch each other, whether for good or bad. Those boys who bullied me as a child have had just as much of a profound impact on my life, in a much different way, as the parents and teachers who comforted and loved me and encouraged me to be my best self. The difficult relationships we endure have value, as do the most positive ones. They all teach us how much we affect each other.

What I hope I take away from this book most—and you, too—is that I am an imperfect human being who will always encounter challenges, triumphs, celebration and sorrow along the road of life. I am a work in progress, and I always will be. I will never be perfect, as this book will not, and I needed to realize both to move on in my life. But I have so much to be thankful for and proud of. Yes, I have a spirit of fear, even when the Bible tells me God didn't give me that spirit. But I also carry with me my faith, my family and a whole lot of great food!

Matthew T. Tessnear

ABOUT THE AUTHOR

Matthew Tessnear is a writer, foodie and former journalist. This is his first full-length book. He is also the author and illustrator of the children's book, *The Monkey & The Bear*. He lives in North Carolina with his wife, Molly, with whom he publishes a collection of favorite American South recipes and restaurants at FoodieScore.Blog. Find him on Twitter and Instagram @MatthewTessnear.

www.ingramcontent.com/pod-product-compliance
Lightning Source LLC
Chambersburg PA
CBHW070202100426
42743CB00013B/3016